What Is Knowledge?

HARPER ESSAYS IN PHILOSOPHY

Edited by Arthur C. Danto

Arthur C. Danto	WHAT PHILOSOPHY IS
Norwood Russell Hanson	OBSERVATION AND EXPLANATION
Jerrold J. Katz	THE UNDERLYING REALITY OF LANGUAGE AND ITS PHILOSOPHICAL IMPORT
Norman Malcolm	PROBLEMS OF MIND
David Pears	WHAT IS KNOWLEDGE?
Hilary Putnam	PHILOSOPHY OF LOGIC
B. A. O. Williams	MORALITY
Robert Paul Wolff	IN DEFENSE OF ANARCHISM
Richard Wollheim	ART AND ITS OBJECTS

What Is Knowledge?

David Pears

HARPER TORCHBOOKS
Harper & Row, Publishers
New York, Evanston, San Francisco, London

 For information address Harper & Row, Publishers, Inc., 49 East 33rd Street, New York, N.Y. 10016. Published simultaneously in Canada by Fitzhenry & Whiteside Limited, Toronto.

First HARPER TORCHBOOK edition published 1971.

LIBRARY OF CONGRESS CATALOG CARD NUMBER: 73-152347

STANDARD BOOK NUMBER: 06-131586-9

Preface

In this essay many questions are raised, but few are answered. It is intended as an introduction to the theory of knowledge. But it might also serve more generally as an introduction to philosophy, because one way of approaching philosophy is to reflect on the question "What is knowledge?" If, like Descartes, I ask myself how much I really know, I cannot answer that question until I know what counts as knowledge. What are the standards? Are they always the same, or do they vary with different kinds of knowledge according to the subject matter? Perhaps it also makes a difference what sort of person is making the claim to knowledge and in what kind of context. Sometimes we might use a very high standard in assessing a claim, but at other times great rigor would be out of place.

There is, of course, no simple answer to the question what knowledge is. The problem divides like the roots of a tree. You take what appears to be a single big issue, and connected questions come up at surprisingly distant places. If I try to say how much I really know, one possibility that has to be considered is that scepticism deserves to be more popular than it is. An examination of scepticism, at least in its most extreme forms, is bound to lead us to one of the opposed types of theory, phenomenalism. When the sceptic maintains that we can never penetrate the screen of phenomena—for example, our own sense data—and discover what lies beyond them, the phenomenalist retorts that this is because there is nothing beyond them: the phenomena *are* reality. There is also a third possibility—that something discoverable lies beyond the phenomena.

This particular controversy is described in this essay in more detail than others, because it is the way to understanding so much of Western philosophy since the Renaissance. The rapid expansion of science inevitably has made people ask themselves how reliable a recording instrument the human intellect with its five senses is, and what its limits are. Moreover, the triangular confrontation of sceptics, phenomenalists and the third party has persisted in this century, and it provides us with a way of getting to understand the linguistic turn that philosophy has taken since 1900. For the same arguments, which used to be presented in psychological guise, are now presented in linguistic guise, and so it is possible to see how much difference is made by these two modes of presentation, and how the new way of doing philosophy is related to the old way.

Many other questions are raised, but none are pursued so far. My main intention has been to exhibit connections, and to show how many of the traditional problems of philosophy radiate outwards from the central question "What is knowledge?" So I have placed more emphasis on those traditional problems, and less—perhaps too little—on the analysis of ordinary conversational claims to knowledge. But a list of omissions would be at least as long as a table of contents, and perhaps neither is needed for this kind of introductory essay, which may speak for itself.

DAVID PEARS

Cassis
1964

What Is Knowledge?

I.

A theory of knowledge is an answer to the question "What is knowledge?" This question, like many which are asked by philosophers, sounds very simple. We all know, at least roughly, what knowledge is. But difficulties appear the moment that we begin to fill in the details. For instance, what is the opposite of knowledge? Is it simply not knowing something and not even thinking that one knows it, or is it thinking that one knows it when one does not? And, whichever it is, what is not knowing? Is it the mental void that a person feels when he has no idea what the answer to a question is? Or is it something more positive than this? Perhaps he has an answer, but it is a false one. Or maybe it is true, but only a lucky guess.

Whichever way we turn, we are going to be involved in complications. Yet the question "What is knowledge?" seems so simple. This beguiling simplicity, which is characteristic of philosophical questions, often produces an unfortunate effect. When people find that the subject is more complicated than the question suggested, they naturally want to systematize it and arrange it in an orderly way. But this cannot be done properly before the complications have been examined. If the subject were scientific instead of philosophical, nobody would feel impatient at the delay. For in science it is obvious that theories have to wait for facts. A taxonomist would be mad to construct a system of classification before the field-work had been done. But in philosophy, because the subject has always been part of their lives, people expect to make more rapid progress. This expectation and its disappointment are well dramatized by Plato in many of his earlier dialogues.

One way of trying to impose premature order on the phenomena would be to say that knowledge is a state of mind which is either present or absent, just as fever is a state of the body which is either present or absent. But this simple answer will not do. For a person can have a fever, or even a neurosis, without having any idea that he has them, but he cannot know something without having any idea that he knows it—or, at least, if he does, there has to be a very special explanation; whereas, in the other cases, he may simply not know what a fever or a neurosis is, or even not know that he is in any unusual state. Nevertheless, it would be useful to remember the thesis that knowledge is a state of mind, and to treat it as Socrates treated the first answers of his interlocutors in Plato's dialogues. Certainly it will not do as it stands. But how much will it have to be modified when we look more closely at the details?

The question "What is knowledge?" has another

characteristic which is shared by many philosophical questions. When it was first asked, it was closely connected with life, and yet, as the answer to it unrolled, the connection became more and more remote. People asked it as soon as they had enough time to reflect, and the answer, or at least the beginning of the answer, made a difference in their lives. For it is natural to like knowing, and salutary to be reminded of the difference between really knowing and only seeming to know. Scepticism, in its early Greek form, has always done more good than harm. The theory of knowledge continues to have a beneficial effect, but only in its early stages. For its more elaborate and detailed developments have very little influence on people's lives. Of course, knowledge about knowledge, like any other type of knowledge, may be worth pursuing for its own sake. But here, as often in philosophy, the gradual detachment of the subject from everyday life can be baffling and frustrating if it is not accepted at the beginning as the inevitable consequence of its difficulty.

The problem of knowledge has another important characteristic which it shares with a certain number of other philosophical problems. That is, that it is so general that it includes itself in its own scope. For I can know, or not know what knowledge is. The problem of truth, which is, of course, closely connected with the problem of knowledge, exhibits the same characteristic. A theory of truth can itself be true or false, and so applies to itself. This kind of problem is obviously likely to be especially difficult.

In the case of knowledge, there is not only the complication that I can know in general what knowledge is; there is also the complication which was mentioned just now, that, in a particular case, my knowledge that something is so can scarcely exist without my having any idea that it exists, and usually I will know, or think I know that it is knowledge. It is precisely for this reason that scepticism is salutary. For if I know what knowledge is in general, I can ask myself whether this particular piece of what I am inclined to regard as knowledge really is knowledge. But this complication produces difficulties. If I know something, ought I to know that I know it, and know that I know that I know it? Where will this stop? Does the mental state at each step have to be examined independently and recognized as knowledge? Or is it enough to make sure of knowledge at the first step, because that will settle what happens at each subsequent step? It is difficult to do justice to the reflexiveness of knowledge without extravagance. Can knowledge really be like a system of mirrors, the first one reflecting the object, and the second one the first with its reflection of the object, and so on?

Before we try to answer these questions, or indeed any others about knowledge, we should ascertain the facts that the theory has to fit. There are so many varieties of knowledge, and each of them has so many aspects that it is easy to neglect some of the phenomena and to produce a theory that only covers part of the field. One way of making sure that nothing is neglected is to begin with a rough classification of different types of knowledge. How should they be classified? What are the important differences? Perhaps the most striking feature of knowing is the variety of things that can be known. Sometimes the verb "to know" is followed by a substantive, like the name of a person or of a place, and sometimes it is followed by a substantival clause, as it is when I claim to know that something is the case. This immediately yields a distinction between knowledge of facts and knowledge of things that are not facts. In some languages this distinction is marked by the use of two different words—for instance, *savoir* and *connaître.* In English it is probably best to use Russell's terminology and to call knowledge of things that are not facts "knowledge by acquaintance" or "acquaintance." There is also a third kind of object of knowledge which is as important as these two, and that is knowledge of method, or—to put it more generally—what a person knows when he knows how to do something. Since these three varieties of object of knowledge are of roughly equal importance, we may say that there are three coordinate species of knowledge: knowledge of facts, acquaintance, and knowledge how to do things. This classification is not final, since each species can be subdivided, but it will serve as a starting point.

Let us now try to answer the question "What is knowledge?" But since it is a baffling question in this brief Socratic form, let us put it more fully and suggestively. What is a piece of knowledge made of, and how is it made? Or, to put this in Aristotelian terminology, what is its matter, and what is its form? The usefulness of this way of putting the question is limited, and the limitations will appear later. For a piece of knowledge is not a product like an airplane. But the question has some use, since a piece of knowledge is a product of a kind. For instance, books may contain knowledge, and, if it is factual knowledge, the smallest units or pieces of it will be statements. What, then, are statements made of? The simplest answer is "Words," and, if we next ask how they must be made if they are to qualify as pieces of knowledge, the answer will be that at least they must be meaningful and true. However, it is not enough that they should be meaningful and true. For a statement might pass these tests, and still be only a lucky guess. So we must impose the further condition that it must not be a guess. But that means that we must bring in the person who made the statement. In order to do this, let us go back behind the production of books, which is a sophisticated practice, and examine the more basic situation in which one person makes a statement to another. His statement must not be guesswork, and in most cases, but, as we shall see later, not in all, it will avoid this disqualification by being based on reasons.

Already we have hit one of the limitations of the question about matter and form. When we examine a manufactured product, we are interested in the way in which it was produced only because of its possible effect on the finished thing. But our interest in how a person comes to make a statement is not entirely of this kind. Admittedly, the main reason for insisting that it should not be a guess is that guesses are less likely to be true. But, even if it turned out to be true, we still should not call it a piece of knowledge on his lips, if he had been guessing. So a statement cannot be a piece of knowledge when the way in which it comes to be made is wrong in this particular way. Hence it is unlike a manufactured product, which, even if it is produced in the wrong way, may still be a winner. A piece of knowledge never breaks entirely loose from the person who produced it. If it is like any other concrete product, it is more like a work of art.

Nevertheless the question about matter and form is worth pursuing. For the meaningfulness of a statement and its truth are both independent of the way in which it was produced. Can we take a step forward and say that any piece of factual knowledge, if it possesses meaningfulness and truth, which are, as we have seen, essential qualifications, must either be, or at least be like, a statement? There is a strong case for saying this of human knowledge of facts. For, even when a person does not express his knowledge in words, but only reflects on it silently, something like a statement must be rehearsed in his mind. This is especially clear when the piece of knowledge is at all complex. How can I reflect that the sun is nearly four hundred times as far away as the moon, unless something very like a statement passes through my mind? Of course, this does not settle the question exactly how like a statement what passes through my mind actually is, and that question is, perhaps, one to be answered by psychologists. But it can be argued that whatever passes through my mind must be, or be capable of being, as complex as the statement that I would have made if I had expressed my thought in words. Otherwise I could not have such a thought. This is a philosophical argument.

If this were a valid argument—and we shall see later that it needs some qualification—it would not follow that, whenever a thought like that one passes through someone's mind, it has to be as fully formed as the corresponding statement. Obviously it need not be, because a person does not receive and interpret his own thoughts as other people receive and interpret his statements. A thought can move from one point to another without passing through every intermediate point. All that is necessary is that it should be possible to develop it completely, stage by stage, in the mind. Nor would the argument establish that, when a person knows a fact, this knowledge must be continually passing and repassing through his mind. If this were necessary, the internal din would be intolerable. But it is not necessary. All that is required is that he should be capable of developing his knowledge either in his mind, or in words, or perhaps in some other external way. It is the fact that this capacity is essential that has led philosophers like G. Ryle and A. J. Ayer to call factual knowledge "dispositional." A disposition is a disposition to do something—in this case to develop the knowledge and produce it as a piece. If factual knowledge is a state of mind, it certainly is not a continuously busy state; it is more like being in good working order than actually working.

The conclusion of the argument given just now is only that a piece of factual knowledge must be either a statement or something as complex or capable of becoming as complex as a statement. Can we take a further step forward from here and say that all pieces of factual knowledge are made of symbols? Broad generalizations are often rather empty, but there is something in this one. For a piece of factual knowledge must at least be true. Truth is secured by matching one kind of thing with another kind of thing; and it is plausible to call things of the first kind "symbols," and to say that things of the second kind are symbolized. Not that symbols have to be like the things that they symbolize, but at least there must be some agreed way of deciding whether they fit or not. If there were no agreed way, language and thought would be impossible. Factual truth must consist in some kind of correspondence between symbols and what they symbolize. There has been much controversy recently about the correspondence theory of truth, but nobody has denied that, if I call a flower blue, my statement will be true only if the word "blue" fits the actual color of the flower. My generalization simply extends this so that it covers thoughts that are not actually expressed in words.

But perhaps this thesis about factual knowledge is

a little too sweeping. For we attribute knowledge of simple facts to human babies and to some animals, although they cannot produce their knowledge in pieces of the kind that are exchanged in communication. Are we to say that they nevertheless can produce it in pieces in their minds? It is not clear what the answer to this question is, or even how we could discover it. The safest course is to say that the thesis certainly applies to the factual knowledge of adult human beings, and may or may not apply to the factual knowledge of animals and human babies. It would obviously be wrong to deny factual knowledge to all creatures who are unable to communicate it. For some of them give clear signs of possessing it, or at least something very like it. The most restrictive line that a philosopher could plausibly take about factual knowledge is that it is only possessed in its full form by human beings after the first years of their lives, and may very well be possessed in attenuated forms by other creatures. This is a reasonable view. For in the evolution of human beings the ability to use symbols cannot have suddenly appeared in its most fully developed form. Nor, evidently, does this happen in the education of children. Indeed, it is hardly surprising that the ability to sort things into groups should precede the ability to put labels on the groups after they have been sorted. For labels too need to be distinguished from one another.

The other requirements that human factual knowledge has to meet must be modified in a similar way in these primordial cases. For instance, the requirement that a person, who knows that something is so, must not be guessing, will often mean that his statement must be based on reasons. But outside the area of the factual knowledge of adult human beings this requirement has to be modified. Animals and human babies need something which is a precursor of a reason, but they can hardly be required to have reasons in the way in which we have them. I shall say no more about primordial cases of factual knowledge, and from this point onwards I shall concentrate on the factual knowledge of adult human beings.

Let us look more closely at the requirement that a piece of factual knowledge must be based on a reason. Suppose that I claim to know that the sun is 93 million miles away. Then there must be a reason for this statement, and, as a matter of fact, it is based on angular measurements taken when the earth is at different points in its orbit. These measurements must be correct, and they must give adequate support to the statement. In fact they are, and do, and so, in an impersonal way, my statement was a piece of factual knowledge. But that does not establish that *I* knew it. If I knew it, then I too must have possessed a true and adequate reason for it, either the one already given, or another, perhaps related to it: for instance, I may have read the statement in a reliable textbook of astronomy.

But the production of a true and adequate reason is not the only alternative to guessing. For instance, I may claim to know that the Italian word *spigo* means "lavender" without being able to base my statement on any reason. If challenged, I should only be able to say "It just does mean that"; for, though this piece of factual knowledge is lodged in my mind, I cannot remember how or when it got there. Yet, if my memory for this sort of thing were good, it would be allowed that I really did have a piece of factual knowledge. There is nothing mysterious about this way of rebutting the charge of guesswork. The human mind is a sort of recording instrument, and on certain occasions the only justification for a statement that it will be able to produce is its own reliability. Of course, we may say, if we wish, that this justification too is the production of a kind of reason. But, if so, it is the production of a very different kind of reason, and should perhaps be called "the giving of credentials." Indeed, if the process of justifying claims to knowledge never included the giving of credentials, it would never terminate. Even when a reason for a statement is given impersonally, like the reason for the statement that the sun is 93 million miles away, it must depend at some point on somebody's reliability, or, better, on the reliability of a number of people. Credentials can never be completely eliminated.

There are some types of statement in whose justification credentials entirely replace ordinary reasons. For instance, if I say "This claret tastes strongly of tannin to me," I can hardly support this statement with ordinary reasons. If it is challenged,

I may say that I am familiar with the taste of tannin, and, if I am visibly savoring it at the moment, that is all that I can say. If I went on to announce that I did not want to finish it, I would be making another statement which could not be supported by ordinary reasons. But in this case, if I were challenged, I would not produce any special credentials. If I said anything, it would only be that I was normal, since normal people just do know what they want in simple predicaments like this one.

Let us now review this account of factual knowledge. Suppose that someone makes a statement. A minimal description of what he is doing would be that he is producing a string of words. But, since the string of words is a statement, it must be meaningful. Pieces of knowledge are made out of words, or at least out of symbols, and they must be meaningful. That is to say, they must either be, or be like, statements. Furthermore, they must be true, and they must not be guesswork. If something passes all these tests, will it necessarily be a piece of knowledge? Perhaps not. For it may be that it ought to pass a further test: perhaps the person who makes the statement has to feel confident that it is true. Is this a strict requirement? Obviously confidence is not sufficient to make a statement into a piece of knowledge; confidence in a false statement or in a guess is merely misplaced. But it is not so obvious whether confidence is necessary. If someone makes a true statement based on adequate reasons, but does not feel confident that it is true because he does not feel confident that the reasons are adequate, does he or does he not know it?

This a curiously difficult question. If his confidence in his statement is much less than it ought to be, *he* will not say that he knows it. But would *we* say that he knows it? We might say "He does not think that he knows it, but he really does know it." The point of saying this would be that he has the essentials but not the complete thing. For lack of confidence is certainly not as crippling as lack of truth, or lack of adequate reasons when they are needed. If either of these were lacking when he said that he knew it, our comment would be that he did not really know it, although he thought that he did.

This makes confidence look rather unimportant. But the fact is not that it is unimportant, but rather that it is normal for people who make true statements for adequate reasons to feel confidence, or, if they do not, to achieve it after reflection. The connection between confidence and factual knowledge can be seen from one of the ways in which we judge that another person knows something. We often say things like this: "He knows that the bridge is safe because he is driving across it." Nearly all attributions of factual knowledge to animals are based on behavior in this way. Such tests of factual knowledge are also tests of confidence, and so they show that the two things are connected. The importance of the connection can be seen in the following way. Think again of the person who makes a true statement based on adequate reasons, but does not feel confident that they are adequate, and so does not feel confident that it is true. Obviously he is much less likely to act on it, and, in the extreme case of lack of confidence, would not act on it. If this lack of confidence spread throughout the human race, perhaps as the result of mutations, people would never act on whatever factual knowledge they really (as we should say) possessed. Of what use would it be to them? Of course, even if people suffered universally from this malady, they could still tell when others possessed factual knowledge by listening to what they said. However, we do not have this resource with animals, and so, if the malady spread to them too, they would entirely cease to be credited with factual knowledge. In general, confidence seems unimportant only to those who concentrate exclusively on the symbolic aspect of knowledge.

However, it is not easy to see how confidence can contribute to factual knowledge in the way that it does. For, if someone does not feel as confident as he ought to feel in the truth of his statement, he will not be confident that he knows it; and it is hard to see how the possession of factual knowledge can depend on confidence that one possesses it. But this difficulty can be overcome with the help of a point which has already been made. Knowledge, as has been pointed out, is unlike a neurosis, because a person may have a neurosis without having any idea that he has one, whereas he cannot possess a piece of factual knowledge without having any idea that he possesses it, unless there are special circumstances which would explain his total unawareness. This point can now be elaborated in two ways. First, factual knowledge is not unique in this respect. Another instance is that a person cannot be in love without having any idea that he is in love, unless there are special circumstances which would explain his total unawareness. Secondly, both in the case of being in love and in the case of factual knowledge, we can give a coherent account of the role of confidence. It may sound incoherent to say that possession of factual knowledge depends on feeling sure that one does possess it, or that being in love depends on feeling sure that one is in love. For why should anyone feel sure of his state unless he was already in it? But the incoherence disappears if we distinguish two degrees: an incomplete one which does not include confidence, and a complete one which does. Being completely in love depends on feeling sure that one satisfies the first degree by satisfying all the conditions of being in love except feeling sure. Full possession of factual knowledge—the complete thing—depends on feeling sure that one attains the first degree by satisfying all the conditions of possessing factual knowledge except feeling sure.

But there is a difficulty here. In order to have full factual knowledge, is it enough to feel confident that one satisfies the conditions for possessing the first degree of factual knowledge? Perhaps one ought to *know* that one satisfies these conditions. But, if so, nobody could know anything without knowing that he knows it, and knowing that he knows that he knows it, and so on. It has already been pointed out that the reflexiveness of knowledge threatens to produce this infinite regress. Perhaps we are now in a position to see whether it can be stopped.

There is no doubt that healthy scepticism leads people to ask themselves, on occasion, whether what they possess really is the first degree of factual knowledge. Nor is there any doubt that, after reflection, they often say quite correctly that it is. Yet these two truths seem to generate an infinite regress. The human mind seems to be a sort of recording instrument which has to be applied again to its own results, and then applied again to the results of that application, and so on forever. But what exactly happens when someone asks himself whether what he possesses really is a piece of factual knowledge? Often he will evaluate his reasons. He will ask himself whether they are facts, and, if so, whether considered as reasons they are cogent. This is one point at which an infinite regress might start; for knowing that his reasons are facts is simply knowing that his statement of them is true, and it might be thought that he cannot know this without finding further reasons to support these statements, and so on, and thus scepticism would become chronic and apparently incurable. We have just seen how this particular regress can be stopped by appealing to credentials. But the trouble is that the mind's reflection on itself appears to generate another more difficult regress. It seems that the doubter has to know that his mind is dealing with the data correctly, and, when he tells himself that it is, he has to know that it is dealing with its own working correctly, and so on.

But is this what really happens when someone asks himself whether what he possesses is a piece of factual knowledge of the first degree? Suppose I say "This claret has a lot of tannin in it," and then ask myself whether I really know that it has. Perhaps it looks as if I have to examine my own state of mind in order to see whether it qualifies as knowledge. But, though this is in some ways like examining my own state of mind in order to see whether I am in love, there is one important difference. When I ask myself whether I really know that the claret has a lot of tannin in it, I do not just examine the contents of my own mind. I review my reasoning, which may be just that it tastes of tannin to me, and review my credentials by asking myself whether I can really recognize that taste. So, if knowledge is a state of mind, it is a state that I examine by looking through it at the way in which it came into existence. It is a state that has to be recognized, not by its present properties, but by its origin, rather like a genuine antique.

This point, important though it is, is not sufficient to stop the regress of reflections and reflections of reflections. For my review really will be in part a review of the working of my own mind. I have to make sure that I really can recognize that taste and match the word "tannin" with the right kind of thing, and I also have to make sure that my stated reason, that at least it tastes of tannin to me, really is a cogent reason—after all there might be something tricky about the circumstances in which I tasted the wine, and both these points of possible doubt are at least connected with the working of my own mind. Much more will have to be said later about these vulnerable points in my claim to factual knowledge. At the moment I want to examine them very briefly in order to see whether they really do lead to a regress of reflections. It can be shown that they do not. For, when I reassure myself about my credentials as a discriminating taster and as an evaluator of evidence in this kind of case, all that I need do is to recall my past successes. No doubt I can wonder whether my recollection is accurate, and there are things that I can do in order to reassure myself on this point too. But this kind of checking yields diminishing returns, and is seldom prolonged. Moreover—and this is the important point—even if it is prolonged, it will not produce a series of reflections of mental states. For at each stage in the check, I shall go outside my present state of mind. If factual knowledge is a state of mind, it is a kind of transparent state: we look through it at its origin.

This brief discussion of reflexiveness does not explain what consciousness is, or show how people can be aware of what goes on in their minds. Indeed it is not even clear what *sort* of answer this question should get. Insofar as the problem of consciousness is philosophical, it belongs to the philosophy of mind, and so need not be considered here. It is enough for our purposes that, in normal cases, people cannot possess factual knowledge of the first degree without having any idea that they possess it. Whatever the explanation of this fact, once it is granted, the foregoing discussion shows that the requirement, that a person who possesses a piece of factual knowledge must know that he possesses it, does not generate an infinite regress of reflections of mental states.

II.

Let us now turn back and take up one of the questions that was raised at the beginning. What is the opposite of knowledge? More generally, what are the kindred states which are like knowledge but not quite so good as it? Can they be arranged in decreasing order of merit, so that the last state on the list will be the absolute opposite of knowledge? If factual knowledge is in question, what heads the list will be the complete thing, as it has been described. Next in order of merit comes the first degree of factual knowledge; in such a case, because only confidence is lacking, we might say grudgingly that the person really did know. But at the next stage in the decline, where reasons or credentials are deficient, even if what he said turned out to be true, we would not say that he knew it; we would say that he only thought that he knew it, or that he believed it, or some such thing. Of course, if he himself were aware of the deficiency at the time, he too would say that he believed it rather than that he knew it. Cases of this kind should perhaps be bracketed with cases where his reasons or credentials are fairly good, and yet what he says is false. For these cases seem to be on the same level as the preceding ones, and our comments on them, though made for a different reason, would be much the same. Finally there is the possibility that a person who is asked a question has no idea what the answer is. In this case he probably would not venture any answer at all, since, if he did, it would be a pure guess. This is the limiting case, in which ignorance is a void. If we imputed ignorance in any of the other cases, it would be a different kind of ignorance. This scale of cases shows that it is too simple to ask what the opposite of factual knowledge is. For factual knowledge declines by suffering not one loss, but different losses in different combinations.

Even this grading of states is too simple to be entirely correct. For it takes no account of the different social functions of claims to knowledge. A person who says that he knows that something is so is not necessarily trying to convey information about himself, like an examination candidate. Very often he will be trying to convey information about something else, such as the claret, or whatever the topic might happen to be. In such cases it is not entirely appropriate to call the sentence "I know" a claim, and better to call it "a voucher." And the fact that it is often used as a voucher affects the scale of graded states in various ways. For instance, the scale suggests that knowledge is belief plus various additions. But, although there is something in this, it would be a mistake to infer that a person who knew something might confine himself to part of the story and merely say "I believe that it is so." The reason for this is that, when anyone uses a sentence like this as a voucher, there is a convention that he should issue it in the strongest form that he reasonably and conscientiously can. For his hearer wants to know just how much he can rely on the information.

A similar convention operates when what is being marked is not the speaker's rational confidence in the truth of a statement, but, for instance, his body temperature. It would be incorrect for him to say that his temperature had reached 100° F if what he meant was that it was at least 100°, and in fact much higher. But there is also a special element in the convention governing the vouching use of "I know." When anyone says "I know" his assessment of his confidence points to the truth of the statement which he says that he knows, and the pointing is conventional; whereas, when he gives the temperature of his body, even if his report does point to something beyond itself, perhaps to pneumonia, it does so only because, if it is true, he probably has some disease, but which disease his hearer will take him to have, if indeed he takes him to have any disease, will not depend on any convention. Of course, the speaker's confidence may be misplaced, just as in the other case he may not in fact have any disease. Nevertheless, when he says "I know" he is vouching for the truth of what he says that he knows, since that commitment is included in the convention. Naturally, when he has issued the voucher, his hearer can put his own valuation on it. But, whether or not he accepts it at its face value, it is essential that he should receive it in the strongest form in which the speaker can reasonably and conscientiously issue it. Hence, when the speaker is issuing a voucher it would be quite misleading if he gave an incomplete report of his own state of mind.

This use of "I know" as a voucher has another, rather queer aspect. One might think that the strength of the voucher ought simply to tally with the speaker's estimate of the probability of the statement to which he attaches it. But the convention does not work quite so simply. If someone fails to light a cigarette because the match is damp, I may offer him another match saying that I know that this one will light. But if I have equally strong reasons for saying that I know that hell does not exist, I might still refrain from issuing this particular voucher. Although it is at first sight surprising, it is understandable that the choice of voucher should also be influenced by the importance of the topic.

The vouching use of "I know," which has been investigated by J. L. Austin, cannot be discussed further here. But, before we leave the subject of factual knowledge, the importance of this use should be emphasized. Its importance is that it destroys a false picture of knowledge and belief. According to this picture, there is a continuous scale of degrees of belief, and then suddenly we reach an entirely different state of mind, namely knowledge, which may even be self-guaranteeing. But, if we examine the vouching use of "I know" we can see that this picture certainly does not fit factual knowledge. When a person's confidence in the truth of a statement increases, perhaps because he finds a more adequate reason to support it, he does not suddenly reach a point at which, and not before which, he must say "I know." There is some latitude about the point where these words should be used, and, as we have seen, the choice does not depend solely on the speaker's estimate of the probability of his statement.

Perhaps this latitude partly explains a rather curious feature of the use of the verb "I know." When a person says, for example, "I know that the bridge is safe," we do not ask him why he knows, but, rather, why he says that he knows. Part of the explanation of this seems to be that his reasons are his reasons for feeling confident, and so for saying that he knows that the bridge is safe, and within limits he can choose the point at which to say this; but they are not his reasons for his knowledge, because he does not choose to know. But this explanation is not complete because he does not choose to feel confident either. Perhaps it could be completed if we explored the difference between confidence, which is a feeling, and knowledge, which is not a feeling. But even then it seems that more would still remain to be done. For we ask people why they believe things, and it is not exactly true to say either that they choose to believe things or that belief is a feeling. This problem illustrates the complexity of the nonlinguistic facts that sometimes lie beneath a very simple linguistic fact.

III.

The other two types of knowledge, knowledge how to do things and acquaintance, still remain to be examined. Let us take first knowledge how to do things, since it is connected with factual knowledge in a straightforward way. The connection is that, if someone knows how to do something, he will very often be able to tell others how to do it, and, when he tells them, he will be displaying factual knowledge. For instance, a cook who knows how to produce a soufflé will almost certainly be able to say how it is done, and when he does, he will be showing that he knows such facts as this: if the product is going to be a soufflé, the yolks and the whites must be separated. Sometimes a person can say how to do something without actually giving an account of the method, and, if he does give an account of the method, it need not be cast in such a simple form. But the simple form is typical, and it exhibits the connection between knowing how to do things and factual knowledge.

However, this connection cannot be found in all cases of knowing how to do things. For instance, I know how to ride a bicycle, but I cannot say how I balance because I have no method. I may know that certain movements, and even that certain muscles are involved, but that factual knowledge comes later, if at all, and it could hardly be used in instruction, like the factual knowledge of the cook. The connection between knowing how to do things and factual knowledge is severed in other cases too. If I can recognize a crayfish when I see one, it does not follow that I can tell someone else how to do it. Of course, it might happen that I could give a full account of the criteria, and so, confronted by a particular creature, I might be able to give my reasons for applying the word "crayfish" to it. But it would not necessarily be discrediting if I were unable to turn my aptitude into theory. I might rely on credentials instead of reasons, and point out that I have always succeeded in distinguishing crayfish from other confusingly similar creatures. Naturally my aptitude would not impress my hearers unless I had a good look at the thing and was in a position to say what it was. But, if I was, my aptitude ought to impress them, and they ought not to insist on criteria and theory.

There is another case of the severance of this connection which deserves to be mentioned separately, because it is the point of origin of a philosophical theory which will be described later. The case is this: there are some words for whose application we cannot give criteria because there are none. For instance, there are no criteria for the application of words like "scarlet," "shrill," "acrid," and "tingling." These words are quite unlike the word "crayfish." It is impossible to produce reasons for applying them in particular cases. "It just is scarlet" I would say if I were challenged, or I might retreat a little and say "It looks scarlet to me." However, since we do not have to produce criteria even when they do exist, as they do for the word "crayfish," our general inability to produce them in those other cases is not damaging. We can rely, as before, on credentials.

The first of these cases, in which I know how to balance on a bicycle without having any factual knowledge of method, reinforces a point that was made earlier. The point was that human babies and some animals possess factual knowledge without being able to express it in symbols. Perhaps these outlying cases looked too isolated, and the account given of them sounded weak. But it can now be reinforced. For, when we turn to knowing how to do things, we find that operating with symbols is only one of the many kinds of things that human beings know how to do; and, when they know how to do other kinds of things, they sometimes cannot put what they know into symbolic form by giving an account of their method. Here, then, we have another example of a kind of knowledge that does not depend on symbols, and so can be possessed by creatures who are unable to operate with them. Nor is this surprising. For the ability to respond to circumstances in a discriminating way must precede the ability to codify the responses, if only because the use of distinct symbols to codify them is itself an example, indeed a sophisticated example, of discriminating response.

The other two cases where a person knows how to do things without having factual knowledge of method are cases of operating with symbols, and they reinforce another point that was made earlier. When the threatened infinite regress of reasons was being discussed, it was pointed out that, in order to answer the accusation of guesswork, it is not always necessary to adduce a reason. For sometimes one can give credentials; one can say, for example, that one is good at recognizing tastes. This too may have seemed a rather isolated phenomenon. But we can now see that it is not in the least isolated. Knowing how to recognize things is only one among many similar kinds of unexpoundable aptitudes. It is, of course, a very important one, because it is the basis of all descriptive language; only those who possess it can match symbols with things. But it is not unique.

It is easy to exaggerate the extent to which knowing how to do something involves actual ability to do it. The words "to be able to" and "to know how to" are often used interchangeably. Practice nearly always comes first, and it is only later that people theorize about practice. It is right that we should be impressed by these facts. For they show how human knowledge can have developed from something more primitive and widely spread among animals. But we should guard against exaggeration. For when the stage of theorizing about practice has been reached, it is possible for theory to get ahead. People knew how to establish an astronaut on the moon before they were able to do it.

It often happens, as Aristotle saw, that understanding how a thing has developed from primitive beginnings helps us to understand it in its developed form. Certainly this is true of knowledge. In this case the primitive beginning is the ability to make a discriminating response to circumstances. In the early stages the response will be a piece of overt behavior. Later, it may be internalized, and stored for future use. Human factual knowledge provides the clearest example of this internalization. When we silently rehearse our pieces of factual knowledge, what is produced in our minds is very like what is produced for all to hear when we speak. Indeed, the internal product is so like the external one that it is arguable that at least in adults it too is made out of symbols. But, having progressed so far in understanding knowledge, we are likely to be held up by a serious obstacle. We are likely to think that genuine knowledge must be internal. For its external manifestations in speech or behavior could all be imitated by a robot. Therefore, we may think, they cannot be essential, and, when they occur without the proper internal backing, they are spurious.

It would take a lengthy excurison into the philosophy of mind to show that this obstacle is partly an illusion. Much has been done by Wittgenstein and G. Ryle to dispel its illusory aspects. Here, as so often in philosophy, the really difficult thing is to see how big the difficulty is. Certainly consciousness is mysterious, and the obstacle is not entirely illusory. However, some of the points that have already been made in this essay are sufficient to reduce its apparent size to something like its real size. First, factual knowledge is dispositional in the sense that was explained earlier. Secondly, when the disposition is at work, it may produce a statement or a silent thought. To these two points we can now add a third: that, when the product is a statement, it is not always backed up by a silent thought. Nor does the absence of this internal backing make it a spurious product. Indeed, it would be arbitrary to insist that the external product needs an internal backing, while allowing that the internal product does not need any further backing. For why should we discriminate in favor of silence? Surely both products have an equally good claim to be regarded as genuine, provided they issue from the right kind of disposition. It is, of course, this proviso that contains the real difficulty. For, as we have seen, it is part of this proviso that, at least in human beings, factual knowledge must be accompanied by awareness that one possesses it. This part of the problem of consciousness has not been touched.

But, if we misrepresent this requirement by making out that it applies only to the external product, we shall magnify the problem in an unrealistic way. For awareness of what passes through one's mind is just as necessary as awareness of what passes one's lips. Furthermore, if we insist on internal products, it will be impossible for us to understand how human factual knowledge developed out of its primitive beginnings. Perhaps the best way to overcome this prejudice in favor of silence is to reflect on knowing how to do things. For, as we have seen, some of our aptitudes cannot be completely internalized and stored in symbolic form; possessing them simply consists in being able to respond to circumstances with the appropriate behavior. If we feel that we are so very different from animals, we ought to reflect on these aptitudes.

What is the opposite of knowing how to do a thing? The answer to this question runs roughly parallel to the answer that was given when the same question was asked about factual knowledge. A person may have no idea how to do a thing; he may think that he knows when he does not; and he may really know, but not feel confident that he knows. But the inferior states on this list are not judged in the same way as the inferior states on the other list. The main source of differences is that in many cases the first requirement for knowing how to do a thing is that the actual performance should be correct; and, when the performance is not the making of a statement, the kind of correctness that is required will not be truth. One consequence of this is that reasons play a rather different role. Another is that, when someone's performance is correct only by luck, we do not necessarily say that he was guessing. For instance, we would not say that he was guessing if, the first time that he got on a bicycle, he rode it for a hundred yards, and then needed a day's practice before he could repeat the performance. In this case the method, if there is anything that can be called "a method," cannot be put into words. However, in other cases, where people can say how to do the thing, we might comment on such a performance by saying "He is guessing."

IV.

The third type of knowledge, acquaintance, still remains to be examined. Perhaps the best way to begin is to ask what its objects are. They vary. One can be acquainted with a person or a place, and that is the kind of object that was used to illustrate acquaintance when it was first mentioned in this essay. Let us call these objects "particular things," or, to adopt the usual philosophers' abbreviation, "particulars." One can also be acquainted with general things like a taste which recurs again and again in different particulars, or with a color, or, if we want more complex examples, with characteristics like indolence or romanticism. All these are what philosophers call "universals": this word is, or at least was, an adjective, and it is understood to qualify the noun "thing." So one way of classifying objects of acquaintance is to divide them into particulars and universals. It would be possible to subdivide these two classes in various ways, but perhaps it will be sufficient for the moment to mention only one subdivision. There is one group of particulars which deserves to be singled out, and that is the group that comprises particular states, conditions, facts, and subjects. For instance, a person may know trigonometry, the facts about a certain family, the condition of the stock market, or the state of the tide. All these are examples of acquaintance with particulars belonging to the special group.

Since it is obvious that there is some connection between acquaintance and factual knowledge, let us first try to settle what the connection is. It is especially close when the object of acquaintance is a particular in the group that has just been mentioned. If someone knows the state of the tide, he must know that it is high, or low, or halfway out, or whatever it may be. The other objects in this group can be spelled out in a similar way. In each case, when the object is expanded, we shall have a substantival clause, or indirect statement, which will be a piece of factual knowledge. To say that someone is acquainted with a particular in this group is merely a briefer way of saying that he possesses a piece of factual knowledge. In order that this should be so, it must be clear what factual question he is being said to be able to answer. For instance, if I say that he knows the state of the tide, the context will usually make it clear whether I merely mean that he knows that it is low, or, more specifically, that it is too low for fishing.

When the particular does not belong to this special group, the connection between acquaintance with it and factual knowledge is less close. It is possible for me to know a person without knowing any distinguishing facts about him; maybe all that I can do is to recognize him when I see him. Of course this degree of acquaintance is minimal, and in most contexts it would not be enough to count as knowing a person. But something only a little higher would count among officers trying to learn the names of a batch of new recruits. For an officer might say that he knew a particular recruit, meaning only that he could recognize him and name him, without being able to produce any distinguishing facts about him. Of course "That is Ramsey" is itself a piece of factual knowledge, but he might not be able to produce any further facts about the man. The degree of acquaintance which animals can achieve is very similar to this. They cannot use names, but they can recognize particular people and places, without of course being able to say how they do it. However, those are limiting cases, and human beings usually improve rapidly on this minimal degree of acquaintance. The officer would soon learn some distinguishing facts about the recruit, and some of them would be facts which would help him or another officer to recognize him. And in civil life really knowing a person involves knowing a great many facts about him.

But which facts about him? This question brings us up against another difference between acquaintance with particulars of this kind and acquaintance with particulars in the special group. For, though at this level of acquaintance with a person there is a connection with factual knowledge, the factual knowledge that is required is not specific. The context no longer pinpoints a single factual question that I must be able to answer about the person with whom I am acquainted. Almost any piece of factual knowledge would do. Much would depend on how the acquaintance began. If I actually met the person, at least I ought to be able to say where I met him, and perhaps what he looks like. But, if I only spoke to him on the telephone, I might be expected to know a rather different set of facts about him. And, if one can get to know a person long since dead, the facts about him that one might be expected to know would be different again. Of course, these lists of facts overlap, and a complete list would include them all. But, if I produce a short list, its composition will depend on the nature of my relationship with the other person, and on how it began. There is no such variation in the factual knowledge which is required when the particular with which I am acquainted belongs to the special group.

Is acquaintance with universals connected with factual knowledge? If I know a taste when I encounter it, or a color when I see it, must I be able to produce some factual knowledge about it? Now knowing a color when I see it usually involves being able to name it correctly when I see it, and the statement "This is turquoise" is itself a piece of factual knowledge. But the interesting question is whether I have to be able to produce any further facts about the color in addition to the fact that it is in front of me. It follows from what was said about knowing how to do things that at least I do not have to be able to produce any further facts which would help me or others to distinguish it from other confusingly similar shades of blue. For in this case there are no such facts, or at least there are none that do not depend on the use of scientific instruments. Moreover, this deficiency does not matter, since, even in cases where I can give criteria, I need not give them. It is enough that I should be able, and know that I am able to recognize turquoise when I see it. I need not even remember where I have seen it before.

It is evident at this point that we are treading in our own earlier footsteps. Nor is this surprising. For there are intricate connections between all the three types of knowledge that were distinguished at the beginning. Not only is factual knowledge connected with both the other two types, but also, to complete the triangle, they are connected with one another. What we have just done was to move back along the base of the triangle from acquaintance to knowing how to do things.

However, the present topic, acquaintance with universals, does take us onto new ground. Consider a fairly complex universal, like indolence. An indolent creature satisfies certain criteria, and someone who is acquainted with this universal is very likely to be able to mention some of these criteria. He might even be able to produce a tidy definition of indolence. That is what Socrates always asks his interlocutors to do in Plato's earlier dialogues. If we regard definitions as pieces of factual knowledge, they will at least be pieces of an entirely different kind from the pieces that have been considered so far. For, even if it is true that this shirt is turquoise, it need not have been, since it could have been dyed another color; but, if it is true by definition that a crayfish is a crustacean, it could not have been untrue unless one of the two words "crayfish" and "crustacean" had been given another meaning, and then what would have been untrue would not have been the same statement. This statement, that a crayfish is a crustacean, is a piece of knowledge of the kind that philosophers call *a priori* and facts that could have been otherwise they call contingent facts. It follows that *a priori* knowledge is never of contingent facts.

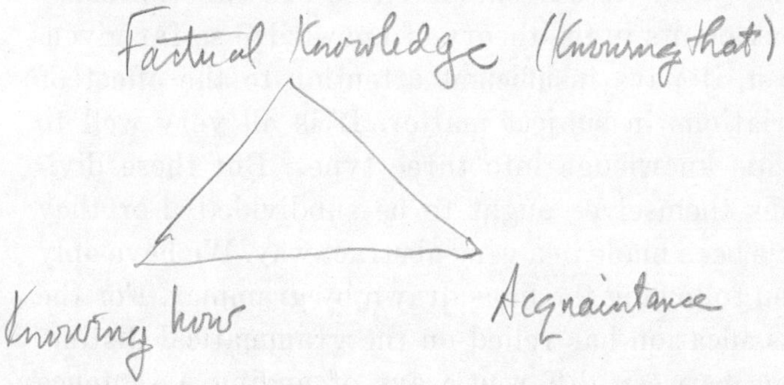

V.

Let this suffice as an outline of an answer to the question "What is knowledge?" It already contains within itself a large number of subsidiary questions which may appear to have been answered, but have really been circumvented. There are two especially weak points in the theory of knowledge so far given. First, it pays insufficient attention to the effect of variations in subject matter. It is all very well to divide knowledge into three types. But these divisions themselves ought to be subdivided. For they have been made in a very abstract way. We have only been following the lines drawn by grammar. For the classification has relied on the grammatical distinctions between different ways of ending a sentence which begins with the words "I know." Now grammatical distinctions often survive because they reflect distinctions in the nature of things. But grammar is very general and abstract. The theory of knowledge could be developed much further if it took account of more concrete distinctions between different kinds of subject matter. For instance, we have just seen that, though the grammatical object of acquaintance is always a noun, it makes a difference what kind of noun it is, because it makes a difference what kind of thing it denotes.

The second point at which the theory of knowledge so far given is vulnerable is its reliance on the unexamined concept of "an adequate reason." Just what is an adequate reason? No answer to this question has even been attempted. True, something has been said about reasons, but only that to give a reason is to state a fact. About the evaluation of reasons nothing has been said. And this is an enormous gap.

The next section of this essay will be devoted to making good these two deficiencies. That will involve a rather different kind of investigation from the one that has been pursued up to this point. What has been said so far has needed hardly any technical terminology, and is closely related to the thoughts of people who are not philosophers. Indeed, at this late date people are so accustomed to esoteric developments in philosophy that it may even appear that it is not a piece of philosophy at all. But that would be an illusion. Even if it were judged at the bar of a superficial history of ideas, it would still pass as philosophy, if only because in the beginning philosophers examined this kind of question in this kind of way.

But from this point onwards I shall say far more about the technical ideas and theories of post-Renaissance philosophers. For I want to show how they grow out of ordinary questions, some of which even children tend to ask. This will involve us more deeply in the history of ideas. In particular, it will be worth remembering that most of the philosophers who will be mentioned tried to give a general account of the structure and limits of human knowledge. That was the avowed aim of Locke's *Essay Concerning Human Understanding,* of Kant's *Critique of Pure Reason,* and of Russell's *Human Knowledge, Its Scope and Limits.* Even Wittgenstein in his *Tractatus Logico-Philosophicus* produces a different diagram, of the internal structures and factual language, but all factual knowledge should fall somewhat within those wider limits.

Let us begin with the concept of "an adequate reason," which plays such an important role in factual knowledge. Now, as we have seen, a person who is asked to support a claim to factual knowledge may not produce reasons at all; he may produce credentials, or he may simply say that he is in a position to say. About credentials something has already been said. The concept of "being in a position to say" has already been mentioned and it presents no great difficulties. The question, what an adequate reason is, is a difficult one, and it must now be answered.

Suppose I say that I know that a signature is a forgery because the person whom I watched putting it on the document was not the person whose signature it is, or at least purports to be. I could hardly have a better kind of reason, since it is true by definition that such signatures are forgeries. Statements that are true by definition are called "analytic statements," and the opposite of "analytic" is "synthetic." This particular analytic statement is, of course, a piece of *a priori* knowledge. Let us now change the situation a little. Suppose, instead, that I support the same claim to know that a signature is a forgery by saying that it is in black ink and that the person with that name never uses black ink. This generalization about his habits may also be a piece of knowledge, but it is not *a priori* knowledge, since, if it is a fact that he never uses black ink, it is only a contingent fact.

Let us put these two reasons under a microscope in order to see exactly what their structure is. In the first situation my reason relies on a definition, but it also relies on the following simple argument: If all cases of one person's signing another person's name are forgeries, and if this is such a case, then this is a forgery. The first of the two conditions in this argument is established by definition, and the second is established by observation, and then the conclusion follows. The argument is constructed according to the following formula: If all *A* is *B*, and if a particular thing is *A*, then that thing is *B*. This formula is logically valid. Nothing will be said about logical validity here, since that is a topic which belongs to another essay in this series. Logically valid formulae are pieces of *a priori* knowledge, and they are needed every time that someone supports a claim to factual knowledge with a reason.

It is easy to miss this feature of the structure of

knowledge, because, though logic is ubiquitous, it is often so simple that it is not recognized as logic at all. If we examine the reason offered in the other situation, we shall find the same logical formula embedded in it. For, when the argument used in that situation is spelled out, it begins like this: "If the person whose name appears on the document in black ink never uses black ink, then someone else put it there"; and thereafter it merely repeats the reasoning used in the first situation, in which, as we have seen, the logical formula is embedded. Another, very similar formula underlies the first part of the argument. For I can argue that this signature was not made by him only if he always writes in ink that is not black. But this condition too has the same form: If all *A* is *B* (not black). . . . However this time the formula has a different continuation: . . . and, if this particular thing is not *B* (black), then it is not *A*. Another difference is that the generalization is not established by a definition. If it is true, it is only contingently true, and must be established by experience, or, to put this too into Latin, *a posteriori*.

How can experience establish contingent generalizations? This is the problem of induction, and it arises as soon as we ask how ordinary claims to factual knowledge can be supported by reasons. For, whenever a reason is given, there is an implicit general statement, and the reason will be adequate only if the general statement is true. Of course, if it is true by definition, it will not pose the problem, since in that case it will not be established by experience. However, very often the general statement will not be true by definition, but only contingent, and then the problem of induction arises immediately. But, though it arises at this very early point in the accumulation of knowledge, the point at which it really makes a conspicuous impact comes later. For science, with all its elaborately systematized general statements, depends much more obviously on induction. Consequently, this problem is usually treated as part of the philosophy of science, and in this essay it will be discussed only in a preliminary way.

I said just now that all reasons rely on general statements. Few would deny that this thesis is true in one form or another. But when it is applied to contingent general statements, there is considerable dispute about its exact formulation. There are two main rival formulations, and the difference between them may be illustrated by an example. If someone watches a stone break a pane of glass, he will realize that the fragmentation was caused by the impact, and the next time that he sees a stone about to hit a window he will know that the window will shatter. This is noncontroversial. Controversy begins when we ask what is the contingent general statement on which he is relying. Certainly he generalizes, because he moves in thought from one case to another. But what general statement is he using? According to the theory of evidence which Hume offers in the *Treatise of Human Nature,* he will be using the general statement that events like the impact are always followed by events like the fragmentation, and he must be prepared to support this general statement by citing other examples of the conjunction. According to the rival theory, he is directly aware of the causal connection between the two events, and so he will be using the general statement that events like the impact are always followed by, and detectibly connected with, events like the fragmentation. Perhaps this small addition to the general statement may look unimportant, an alteration in words but not of substance. But, in fact, it is an important addition. For consider the first time that the man watches the stone break the window. According to Hume's theory, he will not know that it really did cause the fragmentation, unless he has some evidence for his general statement. But, according to the rival theory, he will know that it caused it simply by observing the connection in this particular case without the help of any general knowledge about other similar happenings.

Which theory is correct? The example seems to go against Hume's theory, since we really do seem to see the connection in this kind of case. However, the example is rather deceptive. The first time that someone sees what a stone does to glass it looks as if no general knowledge is involved only because the general knowledge that is involved is so simple and widespread that it passes unnoticed. If he had never observed anything in the least like this happen before, would he still have *seen* the connection? It is easy to underestimate the contribution made by general knowledge in this case because it is difficult to imagine anyone lacking it. The best way to appreciate the strength of Hume's thesis is to take a different case, where people did not always possess the requisite general knowledge, but had to acquire it slowly and with difficulty, and then to ask oneself whether there is any essential difference between such a case and the case of the shattered glass. Try this with the following example. Suppose that someone, long before the seventeenth century, claimed that an especially high tide was caused by the full moon. If he could point to nothing except the conjunction of the two events on that particular occasion, he would probably have been thought superstitious. But, if he had observed that the two things always went together, there would have been much more to be said for his view that they are causally connected. In fact, at that time the only way for him to support his view would have been to show that the conjunction was a constant one. Now is there any essential difference between this case and the case which seemed to go against Hume's theory?

Certainly, if someone feels unsure whether two events really are connected, it is hopeless for him to try to establish a connection between them by *merely analyzing* what happens on one particular occasion. For, even if the analysis is very detailed, the only result will be that, instead of just having two events about whose connection he is unsure, he will have a long list of features of the two events, between any pair of which he still will not have established a connection. If Hume is right, the only way to establish a connection is to look beyond the particular occasion and try to establish a general statement; and the way to do that is to examine other similar occasions. This point might be put by saying that we never perceive a causal connection between two events; or by saying that the connection between them is everywhere but where we might at first expect it to be; or less paradoxically, by saying that connection is simply constant conjunction. Of course, not all connections are causal, and Hume only discusses causal connections. Hence he insists on other conditions besides constant conjunction. But we can ignore the extra conditions required for causal connections, and, in so doing, we shall be generalizing his point, so that it will apply to all connections whether they are causal or not, provided only that the general statements which report them are contingent. For instance, it will even apply to the case of the man who never uses black ink. But it must be admitted that its application to this kind of case, which involves a mind and its working, is much more difficult and controversial.

It is a cardinal point in Hume's theory that the connection between two things, which makes it possible for us to use one of them as evidence for the other, is not always *a priori;* or, as he often puts it, the connection is not always guaranteed by a definition. Hume himself believed that these are two precisely equivalent ways of making the same point, since he held the doctrine that all *a priori* connections are guaranteed by definitions. The question whether this crucial doctrine is correct—whether all *a priori* statements are analytic, or some are synthetic—will be raised in a moment. First, it is important to see that at least Hume was right when he said that evidential connections are not always *a priori*. In order to see this, consider the following example. I say of a footballer that, if he kicks the ball, it will go into the goal. Here the connection between the two events is contingent and not guaranteed by any definition. But suppose that I am dissatisfied with this contingent connection, and try to get one that is guaranteed by a definition. Then I might say, instead, that, if he shoots a goal, the ball will go into the goal. In that case I shall have to wait and see what the ball does before I can say whether he *has* shot a goal. But, if I have to wait, I am not really making any prediction about what will happen. My apparent prediction is swallowed back into the condition on which I appeared to be making it. Yet we must sometimes use evidence in order to make genuine predictions. Therefore not all connections can be *a priori*.

This simple and entirely convincing argument is used by Hume against the theory that the connection between cause and effect can be seen in particular cases. So far, I have been treating this theory as if what it means is that the connection is directly detected; in which case anyone who saw it on one occasion could generalize and predict its presence on another similar occasion. But the theory might mean that the connection is seen in the mind, in the way in which someone might see that shooting a goal is connected with the subsequent trajectory of the ball. And it is against this form of the theory that Hume uses the simple argument given above. His version of it is more elaborate and subtle, because he analyzes the concepts of "power" and "force." But essentially it is the same argument.

When Hume had rejected all rival theories about contingent connections, he had to face the possibility that his own account might lead to scepticism about induction. And he thought that it did. For how could anyone ever make sure that things which had happened together in the past would continue to do so in the future? Of course, there are canons of evidence, and rough rules for constructing experiments and evaluating their results. But his doubt went deeper. His scepticism was not the kind that was mentioned at the beginning of this essay. He did not merely question whether what often passes for knowledge comes up to the accepted standards of evidence. He questioned the standards themselves. This is what is called "philosophical scepticism."

Is there any answer to Hume's scepticism about induction? Some philosophers have maintained that it is sufficient to observe that the standards of evidence are accepted by all sane people because they work. Others, believing that the circularity of this defense is vicious, have tried to isolate some very general assumptions, given which, the results of observation and experiment would at least confer some probability on generalizations about the future. But how are we given the truth of the assumptions?

Hume's simple dilemma might be used again at this point. Either, we might argue, the assumptions will be only contingently true, in which case they themselves will need to be supported by induction; or they will be true by definition, in which case it can be shown that, whenever anyone appears to make a genuine prediction that is based on them, it will be swallowed back into the conditions on which he appears to make it. A discussion of this development of Hume's dilemma is beyond the scope of this essay. Its first alternative was accepted by J. S. Mill in his *System of Logic,* and the consequences of accepting the second alternative are explored in detail by G. H. Von Wright in *The Logical Problem of Induction.* The problem of inductive knowledge, and the whole difficult task of separating its *a priori* pieces from its contingent pieces really belongs to the philosophy of science.

However, before we leave the topic of reasons, there is one aspect of the problem of induction which deserves attention. I mentioned that Hume believed that all *a priori* connections are guaranteed by definitions. Most modern logico-analytic philosophers believe this too, or at least believe something very like it. But perhaps the belief is mistaken. Kant, who took up this topic where Hume left it, maintained that it was mistaken. He thought that there are certain very general principles which are neither guaranteed by definitions nor established by observation and experiment. These would be synthetic *a priori* statements: *a priori* because they are not established by observation and experiment, and synthetic because they are not guaranteed by definitions. How then are they supported? His idea was that they could not possibly be denied by anyone who hoped to give a coherent account of human experience. Their truth is learned with experience, but not from it. Perhaps the most important principle which he put on this list of synthetic *a priori* truths is the one which he believed would lead to the solution of the problem of induction: "Every event has a cause." This third possibility for general statements, which would get between the horns of Hume's dilemma, has seemed to many philosophers to be at least worth exploring. After all, we do sometimes seem to be able to glimpse a third kind of necessity, which depends neither on the way in which our symbols happen to behave, nor on the way in which the things that they symbolize happen to behave. But the investigation of *a priori* knowledge must be left at this point.

VI.

It will be remembered that one of the two main gaps in the theory of knowledge sketched in the first part of this essay was that the concept of "an adequate reason" had not been examined. The examination of that concept which has just been concluded, may do something to fill that gap. We ought now to try to make good the other deficiency, which was that not enough account was taken of variations in subject matter. The division of knowledge into three main types, factual knowledge, knowing how to do things, and acquaintance, is only the beginning of a classification. These divisions themselves need to be subdivided according to subject matter. For instance, it makes a difference whether a claim to factual knowledge is about something in the external world, like a flash of lightning, or about something in the internal world, like the occurrence of a thought.

That difference—between lightning and a thought —is a difference of subject matter, and such differences have been much neglected so far. The first part of this essay, with its triple classification, was entirely concerned with abstract differences marked by grammar. The next part, which has just been concluded, was also concerned with two abstract distinctions, one of which is marked by grammar and the other of which is not. The one which is marked by grammar is the distinction between pieces of knowledge which are general statements and pieces of knowledge which are singular statements. The other, which, in spite of its importance, is not marked by grammar, is the distinction between *a priori* and contingent statements. Incidentally, why is grammar so capricious?

Singular statements may be about an enormous variety of different things. Perhaps the first type to be examined ought to be singular statements based on the speaker's present use of one or more of his five senses. For instance, looking out of a window, he might say "There is a flash of lightning." Let us call such statements "singular perceptual statements" or, for the sake of brevity, "perceptual statements." These statements ought to be examined first, because they come first in the order in which knowledge is accumulated. Nobody could establish a contingent general statement about the external world if he had not yet established any singular perceptual statements.

These statements raise many problems—in fact, so many that, before we plunge into the mêlée of theories of perception, it would be as well to provide ourselves with some guiding lines. Now there are two main lines which run through all philosophical discussions of perception. Each of the two begins with ordinary scepticism, and can lead to philosophical scepticism about the senses. The example given just now may be used to illustrate the difference between the two lines. Suppose that someone asks himself whether that really is a flash of lightning, and not just a tricky reflection on the inside of the window pane, or even some purely internal effect of the kind experienced by alcoholics or people in delirium. Then he might take the following line: "Even if I do not know that it is a flash of lightning, at least I know that it looks like a flash of lightning to me." If he took this line, he would only be qualifying his original claim, without changing its subject; he would only be making a more cautious claim about whatever it was out there. This kind of caution has its place in life. It would turn into philosophical scepticism only if the doubt were generalized and perceptual statements of the unqualified kind were never allowed to be justified, and never counted as pieces of knowledge. That is the first of the two lines.

If he took the second line, he would begin, as before, by wondering whether it really was a flash of lightning. But this time his doubt would take a different form. "Maybe" he would say "I did not really see a flash of lightning at all, and ought not to claim that I know it occurred. For all I really saw was some effect of the supposed flash, perhaps the light rays from it; or maybe not even them, but only my own retinal image; or, to retreat still further, only something in my mind." If he took this line, he would not just be qualifying his original claim without changing its subject. For at each stage in his retreat to firmer ground, the subject about which he was prepared to make a claim would be different. "At least I know that the light rays formed the right pattern, or that my retinal image was the right shape, or that what occurred in my mind was of the right kind." If he generalized his doubt and maintained that nobody was ever justified in making perceptual statements about things like flashes of lightning, his scepticism would become philosophical. But it would be a slightly different form of philosophical scepticism, because it would depend on choosing something that occurs in the actual process of perception and maintaining that the only things that people ever really perceive are things of that chosen kind. It would seem to follow that, when people claim to know something about things that lie further out beyond the chosen things, their claims to knowledge are never justified. For instance, suppose, for the sake of simplicity, that people had only one sense, namely sight; then, if retinal images were chosen as the only thing that people ever really see, it would seem to follow that nobody could ever be justified in making perceptual statements about things like flashes of lightning; so that such statements could never count as pieces of knowledge. That is the second line.

These two lines of thought are obviously related to one another. A philosopher, who begins by following the first, may well change to the second before he has finished. For he might ask himself "Do I even know that there is anything outside me which looks like a flash of lightning to me? Perhaps all I can really claim to know is that it looks to me as if there is a flash of lightning out there.'' And this might lead him over onto the second line. But they can be followed separately, and, if they are, their ultimate destinations are very different. For a philosophical sceptic who sticks to the second will certainly claim that nobody should make even the most qualified claim about the external world, whereas one who sticks to the first will allow qualified claims about the external world. I am not maintaining that these two lines of thought necessarily lead to philosophical scepticism about the senses. We shall soon see that they have also led philosophers to adopt other theories of perception. My point is only that, if they lead philosophers to scepticism, it ought to be to two different forms of scepticism.

Let us keep these two different lines of thought in mind during the following discussion. The aim of the discussion will not be to argue out a true theory of perception, but only something much less ambitious —to provide a diagram of the relations between different theories, and of their effect on the problem of knowledge. And first, since we have blown the trumpets of scepticism, let us inquire whether there are any limits beyond which the anti-sceptics cannot be forced to retreat. Is there any kind of perceptual statement which cannot be doubted? The attempt to answer this question will at least show how far the battlefield extends in one direction.

First let us consider an anti-sceptic who concedes that there are many types of perceptual statements about whose truth even people who are in the best possible position may be mistaken, but maintains that there is one type which is an exception to this general rule, viz., statements like the one that has already been mentioned, "At least it looks to me as if there is a flash of lightning out there." The sceptic will attack this position by asking what makes the person who produces a statement like this one infallible. Let us suppose that the anti-sceptic replies that, in this limited field, his correctness is guaranteed *a priori;* or, to put this more elaborately, that the statement, that he will not be mistaken when he makes a statement like that, is itself true *a priori.* If the anti-sceptic makes this reply, his position is indefensible, and it can be demolished by arguments drawn from the account of factual knowledge given in the first part of this essay.

All that the sceptic needs to do is to use three points that were made in that section. The first is that a piece of knowledge must be true. The second is that a piece of human factual knowledge must be made out of symbols; and the third is that, if the symbols are going to form a true contingent statement, they must match the things that they purport to symbolize. Given these three points, he can easily demolish the anti-sceptic's reply. For the anti-sceptic's favored perceptual statements are certainly contingent, and the speaker's task, which is to match symbols with things, is certainly one in which he might fail. Therefore his success is not guaranteed *a priori.* Nor will it help the anti-sceptic to play on the concept of "knowledge." If it is a piece of knowledge, of course it cannot be mistaken. But *is* it a piece of knowledge? And, even if it is, it might not have been, because the symbols might not have matched the things successfully. If they do match them, the fact that they do is only a contingent fact.

This simple argument is more important than it probably looks. For it can be used against any theory which treats contingent pieces of knowledge as if they somehow guarantee themselves. If the theory is simple, the flaw in it will be easy to locate. But sometimes the theory is exceedingly complex. For instance, the systems of the seventeenth-century rationalists are really attempts to reconstruct what we know in such a way that much contingent knowledge will be based wholly on pieces which are self-guaranteeing. These reconstructions are very persuasive. For large parts of scientific theories are *a priori,* and therefore are, in a sense, self-guaranteeing. Consequently, it is easy to forget that no contingent knowledge can be based wholly on pieces that are self-guaranteeing. There are even twentieth-century philosophers of science who appear to have forgotten this. But in the seventeenth century it was more difficult to see the limits of *a priori* reasoning. Hume's critique of the concept of "cause" was an attempt to fix its limits.

Incidentally, it is not even quite correct to regard a piece of *a priori* knowledge as self-guaranteeing.

If it is a piece of *a priori* knowledge, of course it cannot be mistaken. But *is* it a piece of *a priori* knowledge? This time people tend to feel that they can dodge the question, but they are wrong. They feel that they can dodge it, because they think that *a priori* statements are certain. But if the word "certain" is used in that way it will only be a synonym for "true *a priori*." So about any suggested statement there will always be the question "Are *you* certain that *it* is certain?" No doubt, if the statement is a simple one, like "Either that was lightning or it was not," most people would be certain. But it is only necessary to choose a moderately complex statement, and few people would be able to say straight off whether it was true *a priori* or not, and there are some formulae whose status nobody knows for sure. However, there is a sense in which a piece of *a priori* knowledge can be said to be self-guaranteeing. For at least it is not necessary to check it by finding out whether its symbols match the things that they purport to symbolize. In the example just given it does not matter what lightning is, and the words "either," "or," and "not" do not stand for things at all. This characteristic of *a priori* statements might be described by saying that the conditions of their truth lie within themselves, or that their truth is guaranteed internally.

But that was a digression. We left the anti-sceptic about perceptual statements in an untenable defensive position. Could he do better for himself by adopting a different defense? Suppose that he maintains that, when anyone makes a statement like "At least it looks to me as if there is a flash of lightning out there," it is contingently true that he will never be mistaken. This position is quite different. The vulnerable thesis, that a mistake is inconceivable, has been abandoned, and so the anti-sceptic's strategy is more promising. Nevertheless he will have to make a further concession. For his contingent general statement just is not true as it stands. People do sometimes make mistakes even when they produce these highly qualified perceptual statements. In the example just given, if the speaker had paid closer attention, he might have said that it looked to him as if there were a reflection on the inside of the window pane. True, it is often easier to match symbols with appearances than it is to match them with reality. But, though it is easier, there is no reason to suppose that it is always done successfully.

At this point the anti-sceptic will have to make a second change in his strategy. He will have to admit that mistakes do sometimes occur even when people confine themselves to these highly qualified perceptual statements, but he may maintain that they will only be purely verbal mistakes. But what exactly is a purely verbal mistake? Usually, when we describe a mistake as purely verbal, we mean that the speaker knew the correct answer, but unfortunately produced the wrong words, perhaps through a slip of the tongue, or perhaps because he could not think of the right words. Our implication, to put it rather roughly and approximately, is that a piece of factual knowledge is produced in two stages: first, in the person's mind, the right thought is fitted to the things, and secondly, on his lips, the right sentence is fitted to the thought. So, if a mistake is purely verbal, at least the underlying thought was correct. But then of course there has to be some way of establishing that the underlying thought *was* correct. For, as we have seen, in cases like this a thought is only another kind of symbolic product, and, if it is going to qualify as a piece of knowledge, its symbols too must pass the matching test. So, to return to the anti-sceptic's favored type of perceptual statement, the question that has to be asked is this: Whenever one of these statements is mistaken, will the person who made it always have another symbolic product in his mind which will not be mistaken? Or rather, since knowledge is dispositional, it would be sufficient if he always had the capacity to produce a correct statement or thought. If he always has this capacity, the anti-sceptic will be right in maintaining that such mistakes are always purely verbal. But, in fact, it is very doubtful whether he is right. However, it would take too long to settle this question. Many more examples would have to be examined, and much finer distinctions would have to be drawn.

Anyway the anti-sceptic need not have adopted this particular strategy. For, in order to combat scepticism about perceptual knowledge, it is not necessary to demonstrate that all perceptual knowledge is founded on one favored type of perceptual statement about whose truth the speaker at the time can be infallibly certain. That is to say, it is not necessary to show that the usual standards of absolute certainty are always exceeded in this one type of case. If it were necessary, of course the sceptic would win, since the requirement, as we have just seen, cannot possibly be met. But we can reverse the verdict by saying that the standard of absolute certainty is not so high, and the case for total scepticism is not so easy to make, if indeed it can be made at all. Moreover, it may not even be necessary that absolute certainty, judged by ordinary standards, should always be attained about perceptual statements of one favored type. Perhaps the idea behind the metaphor of "foundations" is an illusion. It may be impossible to reconstruct perceptual knowledge in such a way that all its pieces are built up from foundations of a single kind, all rising from one special type of perceptual statement about which we can at least feel more certain than about any other type. The structure of perceptual knowledge may not be so like the structure of a building. There may be nothing really analogous to the downward lines of increasing strength dictated by gravity.

Even if the anti-sceptic does attempt to find a single favored type of perceptual statement, about which we can be more certain than about any other, he need not confine himself to this attempt. He can fight back and refuse to concede that this kind of carping examination of perceptual knowledge has to end in philosophical scepticism even about the external world. For there are several ways in which he can still avoid that destination. Consider again the statement "There is a flash of lightning," made by someone actually looking out of a window. The anti-sceptic could maintain that, although this statement does not belong to the favored class of perceptual statements, it can be adequately supported by others which do belong to the favored class, for instance, by the statement "At least it looks to me as if there is a flash of lightning out there." He could allow the speaker to offer the favored statement as a reason for the unfavored statement, and so to claim to know that the unfavored statement is true.

As a matter of fact, many philosophers have tried to avoid scepticism about the external world in this kind of way. In order to see what kind of theory of perception this produces, it would be a help to recall the distinction between the two lines along which the initial doubt might have developed. One line, which I have just been following up, leads to qualification of the original statement, but not to any change of subject. The other line, about which little has been said so far, leads to a statement about an entirely different kind of thing, perhaps about a retinal image, or even about something in the mind. Let us now take up this second line, since philosophers of the seventeenth and eighteenth centuries usually followed it, and we shall understand their theories better if we are guided by it.

Locke, Berkeley, and Hume, who all followed this line, agreed in maintaining that the favored class of perceptual statements are about a special kind of thing in the mind, which the first two called "ideas," and the third called "impressions." It would take too long to determine what kind of thing they meant, and it may even be that they did not mean anything very precise. So I shall treat the words "idea" and "impression" like algebraic symbols in unsolved equations. Whatever kind of thing they meant, it was supposed to be the subject of the most favored perceptual statements. At this point their three theories diverge, and each illustrates one of the three main developments that are possible here. Hume was a kind of sceptic about the external world. He maintained that claims to knowledge about it cannot be defended by reason. True, he conceded that the nonrational part of human nature makes us believe statements about the external world which we cannot properly claim to know. But that is another matter. Reason, he thinks, is no help at this point.

Locke and Berkeley drew a different conclusion. They both maintained that claims to knowledge about the external world are rationally defensible. They differed only about the way in which the favored facts, which, according to them, are adduced as reasons, are connected with the facts that people claim to know about the external world. Locke thought that the connection was contingent, like the connection between airplanes and the shadows they cast on the ground. It is conceivable that swiftly moving dark patches should appear on the ground without anything in the sky to cause them, but as a matter of contingent fact this does not happen. Consequently, whenever we see such a patch, we can infer that there is an airplane above, and the general statement which backs up this inference is contingent. Locke thought that the connection between the favored facts about "ideas" and the facts which people claim to know about the external world was just like this.

Berkeley did not see how that could be right. For, according to the second line of thought, which they all three followed, it is not only that "ideas" or "impressions" are the only things about which we can make perceptual statements of which we may feel really sure—worse, they are the only things that we ever perceive at all. It is as if we never saw the airplanes, but only the shadows from which we inferred their presence in the sky. But, if this were the situation, any inference to anything lying beyond the ideas would be pure speculation. Berkeley thought that such speculation was illicit, and that the true account of the connection between statements about "ideas" and statements about things in the external world was quite different. He maintained that the connection was guaranteed by a very simple definition: The external world is, by definition, simply the sum total of "ideas," both those in human minds and those in the mind of God. This is the sort of paradox that makes the mind reel, but I think that our earlier discussion of reasons and general statements is enough to show that, given the common starting point of the three philosophers, it would be difficult to find any other way of escaping the dilemma between Locke's theory and scepticism about the external world.

It will be useful at this point to introduce some technical terminology. Hume's theory of perception is, of course, sceptical. Berkeley's is what is called a "reductive theory." It reduces the external world to "ideas." Berkeley thought that it was possible to carry out this reduction without remainder, since, according to him, his theory gave people all that their experience required. In fact, he maintained that it was Locke's theory, with its illicit inference that led inevitably to worried scepticism, whereas his own theory should produce confidence and calm knowledge. He never succeeded in seeing how paradoxical this view is. Locke's theory of perception has no generally accepted name. Perhaps it should be called "the optimistic nonreductive theory." It is nonreductive, because, unlike Berkeley's theory, it maintains that things outside us cannot be reduced to "ideas." It is optimistic, because, unlike Hume's theory, it maintains that the inference from "ideas" to things outside us is rational.

This diagram of the relations between three types of theory of perception is not complete, since they are related in other ways too, and, in any case, they are not the only three types. But the triple classification has often been used in recent discussions of perception, and it does fit some modern theories very well. However, if we try to apply it to all modern theories, we shall encounter a rather baffling difficulty. As so often happens in philosophy, it is even difficult to explain what the difficulty is. I shall try to explain it by making a fresh start, and approaching theories of perception from a new angle.

Nowadays increasingly many philosophers present and discuss their problems in a linguistic form. I have followed this practice even in expounding the theories of seventeenth- and eighteenth-century philosophers. It might be thought that it would lead to a distorted account of their views. But it need not do so. For it makes no difference whether, for example, we regard the question which Locke asked himself about perception as a question about the connection between "ideas" and things outside us, or as a question about the type of general statement that reports that connection. Consequently, I have used both formulations indifferently. The reason why it does not matter which way we formulate Locke's problem is that he followed the second of the two lines that I have distinguished, and his favored perceptual statements were about "ideas," which he regarded as a definite identifiable kind of thing in the mind. Now many modern theories follow this line, and, according to them, the favored perceptual statements are about "sense-data." Unfortunately, it is as difficult to fix the meaning of this technical term as it is to fix the meaning of Locke's technical term "idea." But at least it is often meant to denote some definite identifiable kind of thing which is not in the external world, and, when it is used in this way, the resulting theory will belong to one of the three types. For instance, the theory of perception offered by Russell in *Human Knowledge, Its Scope and Limits* belongs to the same type as Locke's.

However, some modern philosophers arrive at their theories of perception by following the first line. Their favored perceptual statements are not about any definite and identifiable kind of thing in the internal world. They are only highly qualified statements about things in the external world, like "That looks to me like a small cloud on the horizon." But then what becomes of the word "sense-datum"? When it ceases to denote a kind of thing, one would expect it to drop out of use. After all, it is a noun. But what in fact happens is that it is turned into a kind of adjective, qualifying statements. A "sense-datum statement" is any statement in which someone reports how things look to him, taste to him, feel to him, etc. Now if a philosopher sticks to the first line and reaches this position, it is obviously going to be exceedingly difficult to formulate his theory in anything but a linguistic way. Of course he himself wants to present his theory in a linguistic way. But my point is that, if he follows the first line exclusively, it is going to be very difficult to translate his theory back into the nonlinguistic form in which the philosophers of the seventeenth and eighteenth centuries presented their theories.

Consider, for instance, the reductive theory in this group, which is called "phenomenalism." It maintains that a statement about an object in the external world, like that cloud, says exactly the same thing as a set of sense-datum statements, which includes those made by the original speaker, those made by other observers, and those made by people who are not at the moment in the position of observers. Nonobservers would, of course, produce sense-datum statements of a different form; they would say "If I had been in the right position, it would have looked to me as if there was a small cloud on the horizon." Now how can this theory be translated back into the nonlinguistic form? Suppose that we try this version: "Things in the external world are, by definition, sets of actual and possible sense-data." But this makes it sound as if sense-data are a definite identifiable kind of thing; and, provided that the first line has been followed exclusively, the only "thing" involved will be something exceedingly indefinite and unspecific, namely "the position in which someone is justified in making a sense-datum statement."

I am not maintaining that many philosophers do follow the first line exclusively. Perhaps many who appear to are really relying surreptitiously on the second line, and quietly identifying sense-data with sensations or experiences or some such thing. But my point is that the only way to understand the contemporary state of the philosophy of perception is to keep the two lines absolutely distinct from each other. For there is, as I said, a difficulty about understanding some modern theories of perception. The difficulty can now be stated. It is that we want to apply the triple classification to the theories, and indeed their proponents invite us to do so, but we find that it does not always quite fit. For what exactly does it mean to say that the only things that we ever really perceive are sense-data and that everything else is some kind of inference? If the first line is followed exclusively, it will mean that the only thing that a person can ever be sure of, when he uses one of his five senses for a moment, is that he is in a position to make a qualified statement about the external world.

But is this defensible? I doubt it. For consider the reductive theory in this group—first-line phenomenalism. How could anyone ever be sure that he was in the position which justified him in making a sense-datum statement about the cloud, unless he, or perhaps someone else, were sometimes in a position which justified him in making an unqualified statement about that kind of thing? If nobody was ever in the second, and more fortunate kind of position, how could words denoting "things" in the external world ever get their meanings? And how could people ever learn their meanings? And, even if we do not bring in the setting up and transmission of our vocabulary, but merely ask how it actually functions, first-line phenomenalism fares no better. For there are occasions when it just is not correct to say "That looks to me like a cloud"; if that verb is inserted in order to qualify the bolder statement "That is a cloud," the speaker must have some definite reason for his caution, and very often he will have none. All three first-line theories are vulnerable to arguments like this, which have been deployed most thoroughly by J. L. Austin.

However, most people feel rather baffled when they read this kind of criticism of first-line theories. They think that there must be more to it than that. And, of course, there is. For first-line theories very often rely surreptitiously on the second line, and, if sense-data really are meant to be definite identifiable things in the internal world, the position will be quite different, and reminders about the way we use words in our everyday perceptual vocabulary will not have the same impact on it. Second-line theories go deeper and try to undermine our ordinary habits of speech. They maintain that we never really see the sun, or feel its heat, or, at least, we never do if these things are pictured in the way in which ordinary thought and language seem to picture them; for what we really see and feel is not nearly so far out. Is this position vulnerable, and, if so, to what arguments?

It would take too long to answer this question thoroughly, and I shall end this discussion of perception by sketching some of the arguments that can be used against second-line theories of perception, whether they are formulated nonlinguistically, as they were in the seventeenth and eighteenth centuries, or linguistically, as they often have been in this century. First, it is important to see clearly what the strategic situation is. The arguments that I shall give are not intended to support one of the three types of theory against the other two, but rather to undermine all three by demolishing the assumptions which they share. Incidentally, this is the strategy of those who argue against first-line theories in Austin's way. But that controversy is much simpler, since the variety of possible first-line theories is not nearly as great as the variety of possible second-line theories.

What creates the variety of second-line theories is the wide range of choice between different kinds of things in the internal world which might be the subject of favored perceptual statements. I shall consider only two kinds of things which might be chosen. First, in the case of sight, a philosopher following the second line might retreat into the mind. He might say that the man looking out of the window could not really see the lightning, but only, at the most, a pattern of light and darkness on the window-pane; and really not even that, but only, at the most, his own retinal image; and really not even that, but only, at the most, and this time also at the very last ditch, an image in his mind. This, I think, is what Berkeley meant when he applied the word "idea" to the objects of sight. Secondly, in the case of the perception of radiated heat, a philosopher following the second line might retreat in the same direction, but halt before he reached the final point. He might say that a sunbather could not really feel the heat of the sun, but only, at the most, the heat of his own physical sensations, and there he might stop. Notice two points about the positions taken up by these two second-line philosophers. The first point has already been made: it is that these positions are taken up without prejudice to subsequent developments; the theory of perception eventually adopted might belong to any of the three classified types. The other point is that there is an ambiguity in the phrase "internal world," and therefore also in the correlative phrase "external world." For the first retreat goes right back into the mind, whereas the second stops wherever sensations are, and sensations are not in the mind. Where should the line between the two worlds be drawn?

There are some arguments which can be used both against the thesis about sight and against the thesis about the perception of radiated heat, and there are other arguments which can be used only against one of the two theses. I shall begin with some arguments which can be used against both, but I shall leave some important arguments in this category until the last section of this essay, which will contain more about the private side of perception. What are the weaknesses which both theses share? First, they both seem to assume that when someone gives a physical, physiological, and ultimately psychological account of perceiving, the things which he encounters on the path back from the external thing into the mind will always be like the external thing in certain important respects. For instance, one thing in the external world may well obstruct the heat radiated by another such thing, or hide it from view. But do sensations or images act as barriers in the same way? This may sound a naive question. But remember that what distinguishes the second line from the first is precisely that it treats the favored kind of thing as a barrier, beyond which it is alleged that whatever sense it may be cannot penetrate. If the second line of argument can be destroyed, the first will be isolated and will have to rely on its own resources.

There are also other arguments which cannot be used against both theses. For instance, many second-line theories trade on another assumed point of analogy between the chosen kind of internal thing and the external thing, and that is that the two kinds of thing take the same predicates. This is indeed true of mental visual images and external objects of sight. At least they share many predicates. But, on this point, the analogy does not hold in the other case. For the sensation that I feel in my back when I expose it to the sun is usually a sensation of heat rather than a hot sensation. This small difference of predicate is significant. At least, philosophers like Berkeley lull our critical faculties by peeling predicates off external objects and attaching them to internal objects without even asking themselves whether they will stick. Or to mention another argument which can be used against the other thesis, the chosen kind of thing must be identifiable; but though we can identify sensations when we feel radiated heat, can we identify mental visual images when we see things? And even when we can identify the chosen things, there is also a further respect in which the analogy between them and the external things often breaks down, and that is the way in which they are related to the percipient. Perhaps in the two cases now being examined the analogy holds at this point in an approximate way, for I do see both the sun and (with my eyes shut) mental images, and I do feel both the heat of the sun and my own sensations; but this is only approximate, since the two verbs, "see" and "feel," each have two different uses in these pairs of cases, so that an exact analogy is not preserved. But in other cases the analogy is not even approximate at this point. For instance, people do not see their own retinal images, nor, to take another kind of object that has been suggested, do they see events in their own brains.

It is impossible to complete the catalogue of these arguments, or to attempt any estimate of their strength. Among those that have not yet been mentioned there are several about the naming of internal objects, which are important, and which will be given in the last section of this essay.

VII.

In the sketch of theories of perception which has just been completed, and in the earlier account of factual knowledge much use has even been made of the fact that human beings are able to fit symbols to things. There is no doubt that this is a fact, and an important one. But it ought to be possible to analyze it, and to state it more precisely. What exactly is this fitting of symbols to things?

This question is connected with two very old philosophical problems, the problem of universals, and the related problem of general ideas. The connection is this. When someone fits a symbol to a thing, there are two different kinds of act that he might be performing. He might be naming an individual, or he might be describing an individual. For instance, in a theater the person sitting next to him might ask him which actor was taking a certain part, and he might recognize him and name him; alternatively, he might be asked to describe a particular dancer in the *corps de ballet,* so that his neighbor would be able to identify her. His response to these two requests would be very different. Yet there is a certain analogy between them. For in both cases he is naming something; in the first case an individual, and in the second case the visible characteristics of an individual.

This distinction applies to everything that we can name. On one side of the line there will be particular things, like people, towns, or buildings; on the other side there will be general things, like characteristics or relations (he might have described the dancer by saying that she was the tallest on the stage). It has already been mentioned that particular things are called, more briefly, "particulars," and that general things are called "universals." At least that is the customary use of the word "universal," and I shall always follow it. But it ought to be pointed out that philosophers sometimes use the word in entirely different ways, understanding it to qualify not the noun "thing," but rather the nouns "idea" or "word." There is also another terminological point that is worth remembering: all particulars are individuals, but the word "individual" also applies to universals, like height and agility, so that it will not serve to mark the distinction with which we are concerned here. The names of particulars are, of course, proper names, and the words for universals are descriptive nouns, which, because of the analogy mentioned just now, may be regarded as another sort of name. But it is worth remarking that, though there is an analogy between the two performances, naming particulars and naming universals, they do not occur with the same frequency, for almost all universals that we mention have descriptive nouns assigned to them, whereas very many particulars that we mention lack proper names; for instance, although it would be possible to give proper names to particular garments or to particular sensations, it is seldom done.

The question that has always been asked about universals is whether they exist. But that way of putting it makes the issue sound more radical than it really is. For nobody doubts that characteristics and relations exist. What is disputed is the way in which they exist. Do they exist only in particulars, or do they also enjoy some kind of separate existence, as Plato believed? Even their existence in particulars is problematical. For it is debatable whether the boundaries between universals—for example, the line where one shade of color ceases on the spectrum, and another shade begins—are determined by nature, or by human choice, or, as Locke maintained, by both. Even the thesis that universals should be regarded as a kind of thing is challenged by nominalists. According to them, that is an illusion produced by the analogy between the two kinds of names. Every proper name may name a thing, but, they contend, it does not follow that a word like "agility" names another kind of thing. Of course, the particulars to which a general word like "agile" applies must be similar to one another. But that, they say, is all that is required.

Anyone confronted with this group of questions for the first time is likely to feel that some of them are unreal, because in some cases the alternatives between which we are prompted to choose, although they sound different, are not really different. Certainly it would be wise to subject them to critical examination, and perhaps to reformulate some of them, before trying to answer them. But that task need not be undertaken here, because it belongs to ontology rather than to theory of knowledge. Of course, we do know universals, and a complete theory of knowledge would have to say more than has been said here about that branch of knowledge. But most of the questions about the status of universals make no difference to our knowledge of them. This may sound odd, but the reason for it is simple. Most universals, whatever their status, are presented to us when we use our five senses. It is at this point that our knowledge of them begins, and provided that all our knowledge of them can be traced back to this point, we need not concern ourselves here with ontological questions about their status.

The thesis that all knowledge of most universals is derived from sensory experience is moderate empiricism. Extreme empiricism, which maintains that all knowledge of all universals is derived from sensory experience, faces certain difficulties. For instance, abstract properties, like the properties of numbers, are not apprehended by the senses, or at least are not apprehended by them in a straightforward way; nor—to take an entirely different kind of example—are temporal properties and relations, like priority. However, the empiricist's program has always been to channel as much knowledge of universals as possible through the five senses. Only the method of carrying out this program has varied. Eighteenth-century empiricists investigated the contents of the mind, whereas many twentieth-century empiricists investigate language. But the aim of both investigations is the same.

Hume and Russell provide perfect examples of the two parallel investigations. Let us use the phrase "acquaintance with a universal" quite neutrally, leaving all ontological questions open. Then, according to Hume, if a person is acquainted with a universal, he will have in his mind the appropriate general idea, and this general idea will be derived in one of two ways from sensory impressions. Either it will directly copy a sensory impression that he has had, or it will be constructed out of elements taken from several of his sensory impressions. For example, if the general idea is the idea of "a horse," he might actually have seen a horse; or alternatively, if he had not, he would have to construct the general idea out of elements taken from other animals that he had seen. In the latter case the method of construction, according to Hume, would be to use definitions. For instance, a horse is a four-legged animal, and he would take this feature from some other animal and build it into his definition of a horse. Thus he would get the right general idea by an indirect route, the direct route not being open to him.

Russell's empiricism in his *Philosophy of Logical Atomism* follows a parallel line. When he examines our knowledge of universals, he offers two alternative ways in which it might be acquired. Either the person might have a sense-datum which instantiated the universal, in which case the general word naming the universal would be connected directly with his experience; or, if he had had no such sense-datum, he would have to follow the indirect route, and build up a definition of the general word, using only words which named other universals which he had experienced. There is also another feature of Hume's empiricism which is reproduced in Russell's linguistic version of it. In the earlier discussion of knowing how to do things I mentioned a class of words whose application has to be learned by direct experience, because there are no criteria for applying them—words like "scarlet," "shrill," and "acrid." These words are indefinable, or, at least, they do not have definitions which would help us to apply them correctly. Now Hume and Russell regard definition as a process of construction; it builds up something complex out of simpler elements. But, according to this way of looking at the matter, indefinable words will be absolutely simple elements, and the universals that they name will be the atoms out of which all other universals are constructed. So Hume calls sensory impressions which possess indefinable properties "simple impressions," and indefinable general terms are, according to Russell, one type of logical atom. This idea is part of the theory of language which Wittgenstein developed in the *Tractatus Logico-Philosophicus*.

Theories of this kind illustrate in a clear way the connection between describing the internal structure of human knowledge and fixing its external limits. For very nearly all human knowledge involves universals, and, if it could be shown that all universals are either themselves given in sensory experience, or else constructed in a uniform way out of other universals that are so given, any word which purported to name a universal but which did not meet either of these two requirements, would be meaningless; and so any sentence containing that word could not qualify as a piece of knowledge. This way of plotting the limits of human knowledge need not use the properties of sensory impressions or sense-data as a basis; it could use instead the properties of things in the external world. Nor need it insist on the existence of absolutely simple elements. The essential requirements are only two: first, that there should be an identifiable set of universals with which our five senses acquaint us; and, second, that there should be a uniform method of constructing other universals out of the ones in that set. Given these conditions, it might look possible to plot the limits of meaningful language, and hence of knowledge. This idea can be found in the writings of Berkeley and Hume. But the systematic development of it belongs to this century. A. J. Ayer's *Language, Truth and Logic* is perhaps the best-known attempt to carry out a survey of meaningful discourse. In it he relies on the verification principle, according to which the meaning of a statement is the method of its verification. If there are only two ways of knowing universals, the verification principle will have the following corollary: Anyone who knows the meaning of a statement which mentions a universal must either be acquainted with it, or else must be able to define it using only words that name other universals with which he is acquainted. If "acquaintance" means "sensory acquaintance," one of the weaknesses of this thesis has already been mentioned: not all universals are apprehended in a straightforward way by the five senses.

This way of limiting human knowledge can only produce an outer ring, somewhere within which all pieces of factual knowledge must find a place. For obviously, although it is necessary for a piece of factual knowledge to be meaningful, it certainly is not sufficient. Several other requirements, which were given in the first part of this essay, have to be met as well. These other requirements may be pictured as inner rings, which, one by one, confine factual knowledge within a more and more restricted area. Nevertheless, it is important to draw the outermost ring accurately. For many vaunted pieces of knowledge fail to find a place within it. Moreover the position of the outermost ring helps to determine the position of the inner rings. For the outermost ring encloses all statements which could possibly be related to the evidence of our five senses, and thus, according to the theory, encloses all meaningful contingent statements. But, if one of these statements is going to count as a piece of factual knowledge, it must fall within two further rings—it must be true, and very often the speaker must have adequate reasons for making it; and the force of these two requirements is determined when it is established what sensory evidence would be needed to support the statement.

Since the last war, philosophers have gradually abandoned this view of the structure of human knowledge. It was a view which found expression in many of Russell's books, in Wittgenstein's earlier writings, in the work of the Vienna Circle, and in most logico-analytic philosophy of the 1930s. I do not mean that the work of all these philosophers was homogeneous. There were in fact important differences between them. But they all shared the view that human factual knowledge has a simple, uniform structure. The pieces are connected with one another by definitions, and the philosopher's task is to translate one piece into another, until he reaches a piece that has a direct connection with sensory experience. Wittgenstein himself was one of the first to abandon this view, and much of his later work is a reaction against it. For instance, in 1934 in *The Blue Book,* he attacked the Socratic assumption that the only way to give the meaning of a word is to produce a definition. Language does not always exhibit this simple structure. Sometimes the meaning of a word grows out in various directions from a nucleus; sometimes there is no single nucleus. An account of recent developments of this point would take too long, and in any case the philosophy of language is the topic of another essay in this series. My purpose has only been to show how close the connection between that branch of philosophy and the theory of knowledge has become in this century.

I pointed out, a short way back, that the fitting of symbols to things is connected not only with the problem of universals, but also with the problem of general ideas. What are general ideas? A noncontroversial answer would be that someone who is acquainted with a universal in the neutral sense already explained possesses the appropriate general idea. Now general ideas grow very quietly in a person's mind, and, when they have established themselves there, he is often unable to give a detailed account of their origin. Are the extreme empiricists right when they say that they are all derived from sensory experience, or is the origin of some of them more intellectual, as Leibniz and Kant maintained? Discussions of the nature of general ideas are often undertaken with the ulterior purpose of answering this question about their origin. For instance, when Berkeley wrote his famous polemic against Locke's theory that general ideas are abstract, his assessment of the strategic situation was this: If it were allowed that there are general ideas which are abstract, and not naturalistic copies of the images which, according to him, are all that we ever perceive when we use our five senses, then it could be argued, with some plausibility, that those general ideas must represent something which is not given to us by sensory experience.

But, when philosophers investigate the nature of general ideas, they need not be trying to answer the question whether empiricism, in one form or another, is true. The subject can also be pursued for its own sake, as part of the philosophy of mind. In the last few decades it has usually been pursued in this way. The cardinal question has been this: Does the phrase "general idea" denote some kind of thing in the mind? The psychologizing philosophers of earlier centuries usually assumed that it does. For instance, Berkeley and Hume took it for granted that a general idea is an image which ought to copy sensory impressions directly or indirectly. But, as they both realized, no image could possibly copy all the sensory impressions which it was supposed to represent. For example, no image of a triangle could ever do justice to the great variety of triangles. Therefore the relationship cannot merely be that the image copies the thing. Something must be contributed by convention, as it is in hieroglyphic script. But, if convention is needed, in order to supplement copying, perhaps our minds can sometimes dispense altogether with copying. Or, to put this point in a way that connects it with the earlier discussion of thinking, perhaps the symbols that we use when we think are sometimes more like words than images.

If this is correct, the phrase "general idea" will not denote any one kind of thing in the mind. No doubt, if a person possesses a general idea, many different kinds of things will, on occasion, pass through his mind, and among these things there will be images, unspoken words, fragments of definitions, and so on. But there will not be any single extra kind of thing denoted by the phrase "general idea." Yet the word "idea" strongly suggests such a thing. Precisely because this suggestion is misleading, many philosophers today prefer to use the word "concept" rather than the word "idea." They use it in the following way. The possession of a concept is dispositional, and there are certain tests for the existence of such a disposition in a person, but these tests do not include the requirement that he should identify the concept in his mind in the way in which he might identify an image in his mind. What then are the tests? I have already said something about them, but I did not then connect them with the word "concept." Someone who possesses a concept must show that he is acquainted with the relevant universal, and that he knows how to use the appropriate general word.

According to this way of looking at the matter, the connection between conceptual endowment and linguistic skill is extremely close. Symbols will not only be the means of communicating knowledge; they will also be the material out of which it is constructed in the mind. That is why many philosophers call their method "conceptual analysis" or "linguistic analysis" indifferently. If understanding the nature of thought and language depends on understanding what a symbol is, the question "What is a symbol?" will lie at the center of all philosophical problems. As usual, the question would have to be subdivided before it could be answered. Is the use of a symbol always governed by rules? If so, are the rules dictated by things, or are they, to some extent, a matter for human choice? For instance, do the existing boundaries between universals dictate the rules for the application of general words, or is it really the other way round? Perhaps we project our rules onto the world, and claim to have found a natural boundary, when really we have created it. Or are these two alternatives, although they sound so different, really indistinguishable? Again the pursuit of the question "What is knowledge?" has taken us over into the philosophy of mind and the philosophy of language.

So far in this discussion of knowledge I have hardly mentioned memory. Yet, since the account given of knowledge relies on the fact that human beings can fit symbols to things, it must also rely on the fact that they have memories. For the first fact depends on the second. Indeed, memory is ubiquitous. Without it we should have no knowledge of any kind. If someone knows a fact, he must remember it, or at least he must not have forgotten it. If he knows how to do something, the same requirements must be met. If he knows a person, he must at least remember him, and perhaps his name, when he sees him. However, in spite of the ubiquitousness of memory, the words "memory" and "remember" do not always appear in claims to knowledge, nor in reports of other people's knowledge; and sometimes it would even be unnatural to use them. For instance, if I rode a bicycle every day to work, it would be unnatural to say that I remembered how to ride one.

I shall not stop to inquire why the words are not used as frequently as the thing. Nor shall I examine every type of memory, since a detailed account of types of memory would run more or less parallel to the account already given of types of knowledge. Only one type of memory will be discussed here, memory of facts which the person who remembers them originally learned, and implies that he originally learned, by using his senses. This is obviously an important type, and it is the one on which philosophers, at least in the past, have tended to concentrate.

If someone remembers such a fact, it must, of course be a fact; or, to put this linguistically, his statement that it was so must be true. It is also necessary that his implication, that he learned it by using his senses, should be true. Another requirement is that he should feel confident. Furthermore, his credentials must be good in two respects: since he originally used his senses to apprehend the fact, he must be a good judge in the relevant field; and, in order to bridge the gap between then and now, he must have a good memory. Does having a good memory involve anything more than being able to give a correct report later of what he observed earlier? In an unobtrusive way it does, for the earlier observation must produce the ability to give a correct report later. This requirement is easily overlooked because it is unlikely that someone would confidently give a correct report which was not produced by the earlier observation, although he himself thought that it was; and if this did happen, it would be exceedingly difficult to discover that it had happened. Nevertheless it might happen: amnesia might be followed by a guess which was unjustifiably confident and coincidentally correct. But this unobtrusive requirement, that there should be a causal connection, must not be misrepresented. It does not mean that there has to be a continuous series of mental events connecting the earlier observation with the later report. Since memory is dispositional, it only means that the capacity to give a correct report must be produced by the earlier observation. Presumably the connection has a neurological basis. But we are not yet in a position to use this basis in order to discover whether or not the connection exists in particular cases.

Total scepticism about such memory claims is a possibility that has exercised many philosophers. Whether it can be refuted or not, attempts to refute it certainly ought not to move exactly parallel to attempts to refute total scepticism about the senses. Admittedly, up to a certain point there is some parallelism: for the statement "I believe I remember seeing him put the keys in his pocket" is somewhat like a first-line sense-datum statement; and sometimes, when a person makes such a statement, he will have an image in his mind, and this image may sometimes be regarded as a kind of datum which comes between him and the past fact, rather like a second-line sense-datum. But even here there is not always parallelism, and, when there is, it is not complete.

For he will not always have an image; often he will only have the capacity to say sincerely that he believes that he remembers, or to rehearse this thought in his mind. And, even when he does have an image, the faculty which apprehends it will not be the same as the faculty which at that time apprehends the original fact, for he will remember, or, at least, believe that he remembers the original fact, but he will see the image; whereas second-line sense-data are supposed to be apprehended by the very faculty which is ordinarily taken to apprehend the object in the external world—for instance, one is supposed not to feel the heat of the sun, but only one's own sensations. In any case, beyond this point there is wide divergence. For an unqualified perceptual statement will usually be about something in the external world, which the speaker is perceiving, or thinks that he is perceiving at the moment; whereas an unqualified memory claim, like "I remember seeing him put the keys in his pocket" will always be about a fact in the past.

These differences between remembering and perceiving make certain forms of attack on philosophical scepticism about memory ineffective. For instance, the last difference that was mentioned can be put in the following way: The criteria of the truth of memory-claims always lie in the past, whereas the criteria of the truth of perceptual statements usually lie in the present. From this it follows that philosophical scepticism about memory-claims will survive one simple form of attack, which can be used effectively against first-line philosophical scepticism about perception. The strategy of this attack has already been described. The sceptic insists that a single observation, for example one glimpse, never justifies the observer in making an unqualified perceptual statement. The anti-sceptic retorts that it is incorrect to qualify a perceptual statement unless there is a special reason to qualify it. For the unqualified form of the statement was invented precisely in order that it should be used in the ordinary situation, and it is this use of it that gives it its meaning. The implication of the anti-sceptic's retort is that people must sometimes know, and will in fact often know, that there is no special reason to qualify a perceptual statement. This simple strategy cannot be used against scepticism about memory. For the criterion of the truth of a memory-claim lies in the past, and the sceptic's point is that, when the memory-claim is made, it may be exactly as if it were true, and yet, in spite of that, it may be false. The symbols have to match a fact, but by the time that they are used it is gone. Consequently, the anti-sceptic cannot simply argue that, given the meaning of a memory-claim and the situation in which it is made, the speaker must sometimes know that it is true. Maybe he does sometimes know that it is true, but, in order to prove that he does, the anti-sceptic needs a stronger argument. It is no good arguing that people must sometimes match the symbols with the facts correctly, if the symbols are to have the required meaning. For, when they use the symbols, they might always be wrong in thinking that they remembered the facts correctly. It is this possibility that gives the sceptic his foothold. So the anti-sceptic's strategy must be improved in some way, and various improvements have been tried in recent discussions of this problem.

The similarities and differences between remembering and perceiving are interesting in themselves, quite apart from their effect on the controversy between sceptic and anti-sceptic. Suppose that, when someone makes a memory-claim of the kind that we are examining, he does in fact have an image of the original situation, which was, let us say, an earlier position in a game of chess. Is it correct to regard his image as a memory-datum, somewhat like a second-line sense-datum? If it is, at least philosophers should not complain because this memory-datum comes between him and the past situation, as if they could understand the possibility that, in a better world, he might have apprehended the past situation in precisely the way in which he now apprehends the image. But ought his image to be regarded as a datum at all? This is a difficult question. Certainly he does not search his mind for the right image, like a man looking for a book in a library. But he can use the image as an object of reference, and read off his account of the original situation from it. If he does, it would be something fixed and given, and for this reason it might be called a "datum."

However, it would be quite wrong to infer that in

cases like this images always have to occur, or that, when they do occur, they can always be regarded as data. If perception really is like that—and we have already raised some doubts about some second-line sense-data—then memory is not so like perception. Very often there will be no image, but only a disposition to make the memory-claim sincerely. If this is the case, everything that occurs at the time when the memory-claim is made will belong to the symbolism of the speaker's knowledge, and there will be no contemporary object of reference. Moreover, even when he does have an image, it need not function as an object of reference. For he might be using his imagery in order to rehearse in his own mind a pictorial account of the original position. In that case the image would belong to the symbolism of his knowledge. It would actually be a piece of knowledge produced in his mind, and, if he had been given pencil and paper, he might have been able to produce it in the same form externally, for all to see. In this kind of case, having a mental image is more like drawing a picture than looking at one, and so the image cannot be regarded as a datum.

VIII.

In this essay I have tried to give a brief, and necessarily incomplete answer to the question "What is knowledge?" First, three types of knowledge were distinguished from one another, factual knowledge, knowing how to do things, and acquaintance, and each was described. It appeared that knowledge often requires adequate reasons, and so it was necessary to inquire what reasons are. Two kinds were distinguished, *a priori* and inductive reasons, and their standards of adequacy were examined. The investigation up to this point was rather abstract, and little account had been taken of concrete differences of subject matter. So the next task was to examine claims to knowledge in different areas. The areas were chosen in such a way that anyone who possessed any knowledge at all would have to qualify in them. To take them in order, he would have to possess perceptual knowledge, knowledge of universals, and memory of past facts which he himself had perceived.

There is one question which was mentioned in passing, and which deserves an appendix to itself.

Is the philosopher's task merely to describe the structure of human knowledge, and perhaps to fix its limits, or is it also to produce a rational reconstruction of the whole thing, which would exhibit the true relations between its parts? At the beginning of this essay I simply assumed, without argument, that his main task is to describe knowledge as it is, and I hope that this assumption has been justified by the sequel. But there is no reason why he should not also produce a reconstruction of the system, incorporating alterations which he regards as improvements. For instance, he might suggest that when people use "I know" as a voucher, strictly speaking it ought to be correlated only with their rational confidence in the truth of what they say they know, and not also with its importance; or that, since people so often claim to know things when they do not know them, the customary threshold of rational confidence is not high enough, and should be raised. Certainly philosophers do not have to choose between describing and reconstructing. They can undertake both tasks so long as they keep them distinct.

In the last few centuries several major pieces of reconstruction have been attempted. When the rationalists rearranged human knowledge, they increased the proportion of *a priori* pieces, partly by reinterpreting contingent pieces, and partly by downgrading them. The empiricists adopted a different scheme: they have always tried to show that all contingent pieces which deserved the title of "knowledge" can be legitimately derived from those contingent pieces which are the immediate results of sensory experience. Of course, in everyday life when people acquire and exchange contingent pieces of knowledge, or when they support them or undermine them, they do not go right back to the most basic use of the senses. But the point of the empiricists' reconstruction is to reveal the foundations on which all contingent knowledge rests. Empiricism and rationalism, or rather the best features of each of them, might be combined. Kant attempted this combination in his *Critique of Pure Reason.*

When an empiricist sets out to reconstruct human knowledge, much depends on his view of the immediate results of sensory experience. He may maintain that the whole structure grows out of first-line sense-data, or he may use second-line sense-data as the basis. Whichever he does, he may also insist, like Hume in his *Treatise of Human Nature,* or Russell in his *Philosophy of Logical Atomism,* that the basic pieces of sensory knowledge must only mention absolutely simple elements. Other variations are possible too. But the most frequent and the most important choice is second-line sense-data with no further conditions imposed.

Let us look more closely at the idea behind the word "foundations." Part of the idea is that the less certain pieces of contingent knowledge should be based on the more certain pieces; and part of it is that it should be possible to establish the more certain pieces independently, without using the less certain pieces. For foundations are stronger than superstructure, and they are laid without its help. But is the structure of human knowledge really so like the structure of a building? Various doubts might be felt. For instance, consider the way in which types of perceptual statement are classified before their degrees of certainty are graded. They are classified in ways that take little account of the speaker's position, and none of his credentials. One type is about things in the internal world, and another is about things in the external world; and this second type is subdivided into two groups, qualified statements and unqualified ones. Is it likely that, when perceptual statements have been classified in this kind of way, it will turn out that all the statements of one type are more certain than any of the statements of another type? After all, when philosophers grade the certainty of contingent statements, they are grading something which varies with the circumstances in which they are uttered, and with the training and aptitudes of the people who utter them. For, as has already been pointed out, primarily it is people who are certain of statements, and it is only in a derivative way that the statements themselves achieve certainty. So it is hardly surprising that when philosophers make general comparisons between the degrees of certainty of types of perceptual statement, classified in this way, there always turn out to be exceptions to what they say. For instance, it might be claimed that all second-line sense-datum statements are more certain than any unqualified statements about the external world; but I am more certain that the sun is shining than that the pain that I am now feeling is in my liver. Or, to take an example of a first-line sense-datum statement, if I were looking down through clouds, I might be less certain that what I saw looked like the north coast of Africa than that the airplane in which I was sitting was a Boeing. This is one point at which the analogy between the structure of human knowledge and the structure of a building does not hold. For, if one kind of girder is stronger than another, all well-made girders of the first kind will be stronger than any well-made girder of the second kind.

The other part of the alleged analogy, according to which the more certain statements can be established independently, without any help from the less certain statements, is more important and more suspect. Wittgenstein produced an objection to it in his *Philosophical Investigations,* and other philosophers have argued against it in various related ways. Wittgenstein's objection is difficult to interpret. One of his theses seems to be that, if a creature possessed no factual knowledge about anything except second-line sense-data, it could not even possess factual knowledge about them. This thesis can be supported by the following argument, which may, perhaps, be extracted from Wittgenstein's book. Factual knowledge must be expressible in statements, and there must be rules for using the words in the statements; now it is necessary for the creature to be able to distinguish between cases where it *thinks* it has followed a rule correctly and cases where it *knows* that it has, since, if it could not draw this distinction, its claim to have followed a rule correctly would be unverifiable, and therefore meaningless. But it could draw the distinction only if it could check its own performances, and, if it had no knowledge of the external world, it would not have anything that it could use as a check; for its memory would merely produce the statements that needed to be checked, and the only possible checks would be circumstantial checks depending on things in the external world, and so they would not be available to it.

This objection is sometimes called "the argument against the possibility of a private language." I have presented it as an argument against the possibility of possessing factual knowledge only of second-line sense-data. But, if factual knowledge must be expressible in statements, it can equally well be presented in Wittgenstein's way as an argument against the possibility of a language entirely about second-line sense-data, which would be one kind of private language. The trouble is that there are so many things that might be meant by the phrase "private language." For instance, another of Wittgenstein's theses seems to be that it is impossible for the vocabulary of an ordinary language even to include a section which is private in this sense. This would mean that it must be possible to check any kind of statement about second-line sense-data. If any kind could not be checked, we would not be allowed to rely on our memories for their truth, and the plea, that we had checked our memories in other cases in the usual way, would be dismissed as irrelevant. It ought to be emphasized at this point that, in the development of both theses, the reason why we are said to need a check is not that otherwise our statements about second-line sense-data would not deserve credence, but rather that they would not even be meaningful, because our claims that they had been made correctly would be unverifiable.

Are these two theses valid? Doubts might be felt about the second thesis, because its condemnation of uncheckable statements is so stringent. Is it really justifiable to apply such an extreme form of the verification principle to all statements about second-line sense-data? Must there always be the possibility of a check in addition to the initial verification? In any case, even if only the first of the two theses could be proved, that would be enough to show that it is impossible to establish all statements about second-line sense-data without any help from things in the external world. For, if we were going to rely on unchecked memory in some cases, because we have checked it in other cases, we should still be depending on the external world at some points, though not, of course, at every point, as the second thesis insists that we should. And, if we ever have to rely on our knowledge of the external world, that would destroy the second part of the analogy between the structure of human knowledge and the structure of a building. For the "foundations" would depend partly on the "superstructure."

In the last decade other arguments have been adduced against this alleged point of analogy. Instead of contending that no creature could possibly possess factual knowledge only of second-line sense-data, many philosophers have argued, less ambitiously, but more securely, that the vocabulary which we use when we describe them is essentially dependent on the vocabulary which we use when we describe things in the external world, and that no vocabulary which is shared between people can avoid this dependence. If I say "My left foot itches," even the verb in this sentence does not avoid it. For its meaning can be learned and preserved only through its connections with the stimulus which produces the sensation, the natural reactions to it, the things that allay it, and its similarities to other sensations, whose descriptions are also attached by similar lines to the external world. At this point it is worth recalling the other arguments against theories about second-line sense-data which were mentioned in the section on perception. For all these arguments belong to one group. They are all directed against the attempt to rearrange human knowledge in a way that would allow all our statements about second-line sense-data to be established independently.

The arguments in this group leave the question to which Wittgenstein addressed himself open. Their point is that, even if it is possible for factual knowledge to be entirely about second-line sense-data, at least our factual knowledge does not realize the possibility, and could not realize it without radical changes. The vocabulary in which it is expressed would have to sever its links with the vocabulary for describing the external world, and this severance would remove all possibility of communication between one person and another. Even if what was left was a language, how would we know that it was about what our language is about? Moreover, as P. F. Strawson has argued in *Individuals,* the severance and the changes that would result from it would affect not only the way in which we describe second-line sense-data, but also the way in which we pick them out and refer to them before describing them. At present we refer to them in ways which depend, directly or indirectly, on the identifiability of the body of the person who has them. What would happen if we gave up that too?

Short Bibliography

AUSTIN, J. L. *Philosophical Papers,* Ch. III "Other Minds" (reprinted from Proceedings of the Aristotelian Society, Supplementary Vol. XX), and Ch. X "Performative Utterances." Oxford: Clarendon Press, 1961.

———. *Sense and Sensibilia.* Oxford: Clarendon Press, 1962.

AYER, A. J. *The Problem of Knowledge.* London: Macmillan and New York: St. Martin's Press, 1956. See Ch. I for a discussion of the dispositional analysis of knowledge.

———. *Language, Truth and Logic.* 2d ed., rev. London: V. Gollancz, 1946.

BERKELEY, G. *A Treatise Concerning the Principles of Human Knowledge.* Chicago: Open Court Publishing Co., 1903.

HUME, D. *A Treatise of Human Nature,* ed. L. A. Selby-Bigge. Oxford: Clarendon Press, 1955. See Vol. I, Part III, and especially Ch. XIV for his account of the idea of necessary connection.

———. *An Abstract of a Treatise of Human Nature,* ed. J. M. Keynes and P. Sraffa. Cambridge: The University Press, 1938. (Also reprinted in *Hume: Theory of Knowledge,* ed. D. C. Yalden-Thomson, Edinburgh and New York: Nelson, 1951, p. 245 ff.)

KANT, I. *Prolegomena to any Future Metaphysics,* with an introduction by L. W. Beck. New York: Liberal Arts Press, 1951.

LOCKE, J. *An Essay Concerning Human Understanding,* ed. A. C. Fraser. New York: Dover Publications, 1959.

MILL, J. S. *A System of Logic.* New York: Harper, 1904. See Bk. III, Chs. 5 and 21 for his discussion of the law of causality.

RUSSELL, B. *Problems of Philosophy.* New York: Oxford University Press, 1959. See Ch. V for his distinction between knowledge by acquaintance and knowledge by description (cf. *Mysticism and Logic.* London and New York: Allen and Unwin, 1951. Ch. X).

———. *The Philosophy of Logical Atomism* in *Essays in Logic and Knowledge,* ed. R. C. Marsh. London: Allen and Unwin, 1956.

———. *Human Knowledge, Its Scope and Limits.* London: Allen and Unwin and New York: Simon and Schuster, 1948.

RYLE, G. *The Concept of Mind.* London and New York: Hutchinson's University Library, 1949. See Ch. II on knowing how to do things, and Ch. V on the dispositional analysis of knowledge.

STRAWSON, P. F. *Individuals, An Essay in Descriptive Metaphysics.* London: Methuen, 1959.

WITTGENSTEIN, L. *The Blue and Brown Books.* Oxford: Blackwell, 1958.

———. *Philosophical Investigations.* German, with English translation by G. E. M. Anscombe. 2d ed. Oxford: Blackwell, 1958.

WRIGHT, G. H. VON. *The Logical Problem of Induction.* 2d ed., rev. Oxford: Blackwell, 1957.

Revised January, 1970

harper torchbooks

American Studies: General

HENRY ADAMS Degradation of the Democratic Dogma. ‡ *Introduction by Charles Hirschfeld.* TB/1450

LOUIS D. BRANDEIS: Other People's Money, *and How the Bankers Use It. Ed. with Intro, by Richard M. Abrams* TB/3081

HENRY STEELE COMMAGER, Ed.: The Struggle for Racial Equality TB/1300

CARL N. DEGLER: Out of Our Past: *The Forces that Shaped Modern America* CN/2

CARL N. DEGLER, Ed.: Pivotal Interpretations of American History Vol. I TB/1240; Vol. II TB/1241

A. S. EISENSTADT, Ed.: The Craft of American History: *Selected Essays* Vol. I TB/1255; Vol. II TB/1256

LAWRENCE H. FUCHS, Ed.: American Ethnic Politics TB/1368

MARCUS LEE HANSEN: The Atlantic Migration: 1607-1860. *Edited by Arthur M. Schlesinger. Introduction by Oscar Handlin* TB/1052

MARCUS LEE HANSEN: The Immigrant in American History. *Edited with a Foreword by Arthur M. Schlesinger* TB/1120

ROBERT L. HEILBRONER: The Limits of American Capitalism TB/1305

JOHN HIGHAM, Ed.: The Reconstruction of American History TB/1068

ROBERT H. JACKSON: The Supreme Court in the American System of Government TB/1106

JOHN F. KENNEDY: A Nation of Immigrants. *Illus. Revised and Enlarged. Introduction by Robert F. Kennedy* TB/1118

LEONARD W. LEVY, Ed.: American Constitutional Law: *Historical Essays* TB/1285

LEONARD W. LEVY, Ed.: Judicial Review and the Supreme Court TB/1296

LEONARD W. LEVY: The Law of the Commonwealth and Chief Justice Shaw: *The Evolution of American Law, 1830-1860* TB/1309

GORDON K. LEWIS: Puerto Rico: *Freedom and Power in the Caribbean. Abridged edition* TB/1371

GUNNAR MYRDAL: An American Dilemma: *The Negro Problem and Modern Democracy. Introduction by the Author.* Vol. I TB/1443; Vol. II TB/1444

GILBERT OSOFSKY, Ed.: The Burden of Race: *A Documentary History of Negro-White Relations in America* TB/1405

ARNOLD ROSE: The Negro in America: *The Condensed Version of Gunnar Myrdal's* An American Dilemma. *Second Edition* TB/3048

JOHN E. SMITH: Themes in American Philosophy: *Purpose, Experience and Community* TB/1466

WILLIAM R. TAYLOR: Cavalier and Yankee: *The Old South and American National Character* TB/1474

American Studies: Colonial

BERNARD BAILYN: The New England Merchants in the Seventeenth Century TB/1149

ROBERT E. BROWN: Middle-Class Democracy and Revolution in Massachusetts, 1691–1780. *New Introduction by Author* TB/1413

JOSEPH CHARLES: The Origins of the American Party System TB/1049

WESLEY FRANK CRAVEN: The Colonies in Transition: 1660-1712† TB/3084

CHARLES GIBSON: Spain in America † TB/3077

CHARLES GIBSON, Ed.: The Spanish Tradition in America + HR/1351

LAWRENCE HENRY GIPSON: The Coming of the Revolution: 1763-1775. † *Illus.* TB/3007

JACK P. GREENE, Ed.: Great Britain and the American Colonies: 1606-1763. + *Introduction by the Author* HR/1477

AUBREY C. LAND, Ed.: Bases of the Plantation Society + HR/1429

PERRY MILLER: Errand Into the Wilderness TB/1139

PERRY MILLER & T. H. JOHNSON, Ed.: The Puritans: *A Sourcebook of Their Writings* Vol. I TB/1093; Vol. II TB/1094

EDMUND S. MORGAN: The Puritan Family: *Religion and Domestic Relations in Seventeenth Century New England* TB/1227

WALLACE NOTESTEIN: The English People on the Eve of Colonization: 1603-1630. † *Illus.* TB/3006

LOUIS B. WRIGHT: The Cultural Life of the American Colonies: 1607-1763. † *Illus.* TB/3005

YVES F. ZOLTVANY, Ed.: The French Tradition in America + HR/1425

American Studies: The Revolution to 1860

JOHN R. ALDEN: The American Revolution: 1775-1783. † *Illus.* TB/3011

† The New American Nation Series, edited by Henry Steele Commager and Richard B. Morris.
‡ American Perspectives series, edited by Bernard Wishy and William E. Leuchtenburg.
α History of Europe series, edited by J. H. Plumb.
§ The Library of Religion and Culture, edited by Benjamin Nelson.
|| Researches in the Social, Cultural, and Behavioral Sciences, edited by Benjamin Nelson.
Σ Harper Modern Science Series, edited by James A. Newman.
° Not for sale in Canada.
+ Documentary History of the United States series, edited by Richard B. Morris.
# Documentary History of Western Civilization series, edited by Eugene C. Black and Leonard W. Levy.
^ The Economic History of the United States series, edited by Henry David et al.
¶ European Perspectives series, edited by Eugene C. Black.
** Contemporary Essays series, edited by Leonard W. Levy.
* The Stratum Series, edited by John Hale.

RAY A. BILLINGTON: The Far Western Frontier: 1830-1860. † *Illus.* TB/3012

STUART BRUCHEY: The Roots of American Economic Growth, 1607-1861: *An Essay in Social Causation. New Introduction by the Author.* TB/1350

WHITNEY R. CROSS: The Burned-Over District: *The Social and Intellectual History of Enthusiastic Religion in Western New York, 1800-1850* TB/1242

NOBLE E. CUNNINGHAM, JR., Ed.: The Early Republic, 1789-1828 + HR/1394

GEORGE DANGERFIELD: The Awakening of American Nationalism, 1815-1828. † *Illus.* TB/3061

CLEMENT EATON: The Freedom-of-Thought Struggle in the Old South. *Revised and Enlarged. Illus.* TB/1150

CLEMENT EATON: The Growth of Southern Civilization, 1790-1860. † *Illus.* TB/3040

ROBERT H. FERRELL, Ed.: Foundations of American Diplomacy, 1775-1872 + HR/1393

LOUIS FILLER: The Crusade against Slavery: 1830-1860. † *Illus.* TB/3029

DAVID H. FISCHER: The Revolution of American Conservatism: *The Federalist Party in the Era of Jeffersonian Democracy* TB/1449

WILLIM W. FREEHLING: Prelude to Civil War: *The Nullification Controversy in South Carolina, 1816-1836* TB/1359

PAUL W. GATES: The Farmer's Age: *Agriculture, 1815-1860* Δ TB/1398

THOMAS JEFFERSON: Notes on the State of Virginia. ‡ *Edited by Thomas P. Abernethy* TB/3052

FORREST MCDONALD, Ed.: Confederation and Constitution, 1781-1789 + HR/1396

BERNARD MAYO: Myths and Men: *Patrick Henry, George Washington, Thomas Jefferson* TB/1108

JOHN C. MILLER: Alexander Hamilton and the Growth of the New Nation TB/3057

JOHN C. MILLER: The Federalist Era: 1789-1801. † *Illus.* TB/3027

RICHARD B. MORRIS, Ed.: Alexander Hamilton and the Founding of the Nation. *New Introduction by the Editor* TB/1448

RICHARD B. MORRIS: The American Revolution Reconsidered TB/1363

CURTIS P. NETTELS: The Emergence of a National Economy, 1775-1815 Δ TB/1438

DOUGLASS C. NORTH & ROBERT PAUL THOMAS, Eds.: *The Growth of the American Economy to 1860* + HR/1352

R. B. NYE: The Cultural Life of the New Nation: 1776-1830. † *Illus.* TB/3026

GILBERT OSOFSKY, Ed.: Puttin' On Ole Massa: *The Slave Narratives of Henry Bibb, William Wells Brown, and Solomon Northup* ‡ TB/1432

JAMES PARTON: The Presidency of Andrew Jackson. *From Volume III of the* Life of Andrew Jackson. *Ed. with Intro. by Robert V. Remini* TB/3080

FRANCIS S. PHILBRICK: The Rise of the West, 1754-1830. † *Illus.* TB/3067

MARSHALL SMELSER: The Democratic Republic, 1801-1815 † TB/1406

JACK M. SOSIN, Ed.: The Opening of the West + HR/1424

GEORGE ROGERS TAYLOR: The Transportation Revolution, 1815-1860 Δ TB/1347

A. F. TYLER: Freedom's Ferment: *Phases of American Social History from the Revolution to the Outbreak of the Civil War. Illus.* TB/1074

GLYNDON G. VAN DEUSEN: The Jacksonian Era: 1828-1848. † *Illus.* TB/3028

LOUIS B. WRIGHT: Culture on the Moving Frontier TB/1053

American Studies: The Civil War to 1900

W. R. BROCK: An American Crisis: *Congress and Reconstruction, 1865-67* ° TB/1283

T. C. COCHRAN & WILLIAM MILLER: The Age of Enterprise: *A Social History of Industrial America* TB/1054

W. A. DUNNING: Reconstruction, Political and Economic: 1865-1877 TB/1073

HAROLD U. FAULKNER: Politics, Reform and Expansion: 1890-1900. † *Illus.* TB/3020

GEORGE M. FREDRICKSON: The Inner Civil War: *Northern Intellectuals and the Crisis of the Union* TB/1358

JOHN A. GARRATY: The New Commonwealth, 1877-1890 † TB/1410

JOHN A. GARRATY, Ed.: The Transformation of American Society, 1870-1890 + HR/1395

HELEN HUNT JACKSON: A Century of Dishonor: *The Early Crusade for Indian Reform.* † *Edited by Andrew F. Rolle* TB/3063

WILLIAM G. MCLOUGHLIN, Ed.: The American Evangelicals, 1800-1900: An Anthology ‡ TB/1382

ARNOLD M. PAUL: Conservative Crisis and the Rule of Law: *Attitudes of Bar and Bench, 1887-1895. New Introduction by Author* TB/1415

JAMES S. PIKE: The Prostrate State: *South Carolina under Negro Government.* ‡ *Intro. by Robert F. Durden* TB/3085

WHITELAW REID: After the War: *A Tour of the Southern States, 1865-1866.* ‡ *Edited by C. Vann Woodward* TB/3066

FRED A. SHANNON: The Farmer's Last Frontier: *Agriculture, 1860-1897* TB/1348

VERNON LANE WHARTON: The Negro in Mississippi, 1865-1890 TB/1178

American Studies: The Twentieth Century

RICHARD M. ABRAMS, Ed.: The Issues of the Populist and Progressive Eras, 1892-1912 + HR/1428

RAY STANNARD BAKER: Following the Color Line: *American Negro Citizenship in Progressive Era.* ‡ *Edited by Dewey W. Grantham, Jr. Illus.* TB/3053

RANDOLPH S. BOURNE: War and the Intellectuals: *Collected Essays, 1915-1919.* ‡ *Edited by Carl Resek* TB/3043

A. RUSSELL BUCHANAN: The United States and World War II. † *Illus.* Vol. I TB/3044; Vol. II TB/3045

THOMAS C. COCHRAN: The American Business System: *A Historical Perspective, 1900-1955* TB/1080

FOSTER RHEA DULLES: America's Rise to World Power: 1898-1954. † *Illus.* TB/3021

JEAN-BAPTISTE DUROSELLE: From Wilson to Roosevelt: *Foreign Policy of the United States, 1913-1945. Trans. by Nancy Lyman Roelker* TB/1370

HAROLD U. FAULKNER: The Decline of Laissez Faire, 1897-1917 TB/1397

JOHN D. HICKS: Republican Ascendancy: 1921-1933. † *Illus.* TB/3041

WILLIAM E. LEUCHTENBURG: Franklin D. Roosevelt and the New Deal: 1932-1940. † *Illus.* TB/3025

WILLIAM E. LEUCHTENBURG, Ed.: The New Deal: *A Documentary History* + HR/1354

ARTHUR S. LINK: Woodrow Wilson and the Progressive Era: 1910-1917. † *Illus.* TB/3023

BROADUS MITCHELL: Depression Decade: *From New Era through New Deal; 1929-1941* Δ TB/1439

GEORGE E. MOWRY: The Era of Theodore Roosevelt and the Birth of Modern America: 1900-1912. † *Illus.* TB/3022

WILLIAM PRESTON, JR.: Aliens and Dissenters: *Federal Suppression of Radicals, 1903-1933* TB/1287

WALTER RAUSCHENBUSCH: Christianity and the Social Crisis. ‡ *Edited by Robert D. Cross* TB/3059

GEORGE SOULE: Prosperity Decade: *From War to Depression, 1917-1929* Δ TB/1349

GEORGE B. TINDALL, Ed.: A Populist Reader: *Selections from the Works of American Populist Leaders* TB/3069

TWELVE SOUTHERNERS: I'll Take My Stand: *The South and the Agrarian Tradition. Intro. by Louis D. Rubin, Jr.; Biographical Essays by Virginia Rock* TB/1072

Art, Art History, Aesthetics

CREIGHTON GILBERT, Ed.: Renaissance Art ** *Illus.* TB/1465

EMILE MALE: The Gothic Image: *Religious Art in France of the Thirteenth Century. § 190* illus. TB/344

MILLARD MEISS: Painting in Florence and Siena After the Black Death: *The Arts, Religion and Society in the Mid-Fourteenth Century. 169 illus.* TB/1148

ERWIN PANOFSKY: Renaissance and Renascences in Western Art. *Illus.* TB/1447

ERWIN PANOFSKY: Studies in Iconology: *Humanistic Themes in the Art of the Renaissance. 180 illus.* TB/1077

OTTO VON SIMSON: The Gothic Cathedral: *Origins of Gothic Architecture and the Medieval Concept of Order. 58 illus.* TB/2018

HEINRICH ZIMMER: Myths and Symbols in Indian Art and Civilization. *70 illus.* TB/2005

Asian Studies

WOLFGANG FRANKE: China and the West: *The Cultural Encounter, 13th to 20th Centuries. Trans. by R. A. Wilson* TB/1326

L. CARRINGTON GOODRICH: A Short History of the Chinese People. *Illus.* TB/3015

DAN N. JACOBS, Ed.: The New Communist Manifesto and Related Documents. TB/1078

DAN N. JACOBS & HANS H. BAERWALD, Eds.: Chinese Communism: *Selected Documents* TB/3031

BENJAMIN I. SCHWARTZ: Chinese Communism and the Rise of Mao TB/1308

BENJAMIN I. SCHWARTZ: In Search of Wealth and Power: *Yen Fu and the West* TB/1422

Economics & Economic History

C. E. BLACK: The Dynamics of Modernization: *A Study in Comparative History* TB/1321

STUART BRUCHEY: The Roots of American Economic Growth, 1607-1861: *An Essay in Social Causation. New Introduction by the Author.* TB/1350

GILBERT BURCK & EDITORS OF *Fortune:* The Computer Age: *And its Potential for Management* TB/1179

SHEPARD B. CLOUGH, THOMAS MOODIE & CAROL MOODIE, Eds.: Economic History of Europe: *Twentieth Century #* HR/1388

THOMAS C. COCHRAN: The American Business System: *A Historical Perspective, 1900-1955* TB/1080

ROBERT A. DAHL & CHARLES E. LINDBLOM: Politics, Economics, and Welfare: *Planning and Politico-Economic Systems Resolved into Basic Social Processes* TB/3037

PETER F. DRUCKER: The New Society: *The Anatomy of Industrial Order* TB/1082

HAROLD U. FAULKNER: The Decline of Laissez Faire, 1897-1917 Δ TB/1397

PAUL W. GATES: The Farmer's Age: *Agriculture, 1815-1860* Δ TB/1398

WILLIAM GREENLEAF, Ed.: American Economic Development Since 1860 + HR/1353

ROBERT L. HEILBRONER: The Future as History: *The Historic Currents of Our Time and the Direction in Which They Are Taking America* TB/1386

ROBERT L. HEILBRONER: The Great Ascent: *The Struggle for Economic Development in Our Time* TB/3030

DAVID S. LANDES: Bankers and Pashas: *International Finance and Economic Imperialism in Egypt. New Preface by the Author* TB/1412

ROBERT LATOUCHE: The Birth of Western Economy: *Economic Aspects of the Dark Ages* TB/1290

W. ARTHUR LEWIS: The Principles of Economic Planning. *New Introduction by the Author°* TB/1436

WILLIAM MILLER, Ed.: Men in Business: *Essays on the Historical Role of the Entrepreneur* TB/1081

GUNNAR MYRDAL: An International Economy. *New Introduction by the Author* TB/1445

HERBERT A. SIMON: The Shape of Automation: *For Men and Management* TB/1245

RICHARD S. WECKSTEIN, Ed.: Expansion of World Trade and the Growth of National Economies ** TB/1373

Historiography and History of Ideas

J. BRONOWSKI & BRUCE MAZLISH: The Western Intellectual Tradition: *From Leonardo to Hegel* TB/3001

WILHELM DILTHEY: Pattern and Meaning in History: *Thoughts on History and Society.° Edited with an Intro. by H. P. Rickman* TB/1075

J. H. HEXTER: More's Utopia: *The Biography of an Idea. Epilogue by the Author* TB/1195

H. STUART HUGHES: History as Art and as Science: *Twin Vistas on the Past* TB/1207

ARTHUR O. LOVEJOY: The Great Chain of Being: *A Study of the History of an Idea* TB/1009

RICHARD H. POPKIN: The History of Scepticism from Erasmus to Descartes. *Revised Edition* TB/1391

MASSIMO SALVADORI, Ed.: Modern Socialism # HR/1374

BRUNO SNELL: The Discovery of the Mind: *The Greek Origins of European Thought* TB/1018

W. WARREN WAGER, ed.: European Intellectual History Since Darwin and Marx TB/1297

History: General

HANS KOHN: The Age of Nationalism: *The First Era of Global History* TB/1380

BERNARD LEWIS: The Arabs in History TB/1029

BERNARD LEWIS: The Middle East and the West ° TB/1274

History: Ancient

A. ANDREWS: The Greek Tyrants TB/1103

ERNST LUDWIG EHRLICH: A Concise History of Israel: *From the Earliest Times to the Destruction of the Temple in A.D. 70* ° TB/128
THEODOR H. GASTER: Thespis: *Ritual Myth and Drama in the Ancient Near East* TB/1281
MICHAEL GRANT: Ancient History ° TB/1190
A. H. M. JONES, Ed.: A History of Rome through the Fifth Century # *Vol. I: The Republic* HR/1364
Vol. II The Empire: HR/1460
NAPHTALI LEWIS & MEYER REINHOLD, Eds.: Roman Civilization *Vol. I: The Republic* TB/1231
Vol. II: The Empire TB/1232

History: Medieval

MARSHALL W. BALDWIN, Ed.: Christianity Through the 13th Century # HR/1468
MARC BLOCH: Land and Work in Medieval Europe. *Translated by J. E. Anderson* TB/1452
HELEN CAM: England Before Elizabeth TB/1026
NORMAN COHN: The Pursuit of the Millennium: *Revolutionary Messianism in Medieval and Reformation Europe* TB/1037
G. G. COULTON: Medieval Village, Manor, and Monastery HR/1022
HEINRICH FICHTENAU: The Carolingian Empire: *The Age of Charlemagne. Translated with an Introduction by Peter Munz* TB/1142
GALBERT OF BRUGES: The Murder of Charles the Good: *A Contemporary Record of Revolutionary Change in 12th Century Flanders. Translated with an Introduction by James Bruce Ross* TB/1311
F. L. GANSHOF: Feudalism TB/1058
F. L. GANSHOF: The Middle Ages: *A History of International Relations. Translated by Rêmy Hall* TB/1411
DENYS HAY: The Medieval Centuries ° TB/1192
DAVID HERLIHY, Ed.: Medieval Culture and Socitey # HR/1340
J. M. HUSSEY: The Byzantine World TB/1057
ROBERT LATOUCHE: The Birth of Western Economy: *Economic Aspects of the Dark Ages* ° TB/1290
HENRY CHARLES LEA: The Inquisition of the Middle Ages. || *Introduction by Walter Ullmann* TB/1456
FERDINARD LOT: The End of the Ancient World and the Beginnings of the Middle Ages. *Introduction by Glanville Downey* TB/1044
H. R. LOYN: The Norman Conquest TB/1457
ACHILLE LUCHAIRE: Social France at the time of Philip Augustus. *Intro. by John W. Baldwin* TB/1314
GUIBERT DE NOGENT: Self and Society in Medieval France: *The Memoirs of Guibert de Nogent.* || Edited by John F. Benton TB/1471
MARSILIUS OF PADUA: The Defender of Peace. *The* Defensor Pacis. *Translated with an Introduction by Alan Gewirth* TB/1310
CHARLES PETET-DUTAILLIS: The Feudal Monarchy in France and England: *From the Tenth to the Thirteenth Century* ° TB/1165
STEVEN RUNCIMAN: A History of the Crusades Vol. I: *The First Crusade and the Foundation of the Kingdom of Jerusalem. Illus.* TB/1143
Vol. II: *The Kingdom of Jerusalem and the Frankish East 1100-1187. Illus.* TB/1243
Vol. III: *The Kingdom of Acre and the Later Crusades. Illus.* TB/1298
J. M. WALLACE-HADRILL: The Barbarian West: *The Early Middle Ages, A.D. 400-1000* TB/1061

History: Renaissance & Reformation

JACOB BURCKHARDT: The Civilization of the Renaissance in Italy. *Introduction by Benjamin Nelson and Charles Trinkaus. Illus.* Vol. I TB/40; Vol. II TB/41
JOHN CALVIN & JACOPO SADOLETO: A Reformation Debate. *Edited by John C. Olin* TB/1239
FEDERICO CHABOD: Machiavelli and the Renaissance TB/1193
J. H. ELLIOTT: Europe Divided, 1559-1598 *a* ° TB/1414
G. R. ELTON: Reformation Europe, 1517-1559 ° *a* TB/1270
DESIDERIUS ERASMUS: Christian Humanism and the Reformation: *Selected Writings. Edited and Translated by John C. Olin* TB/1166
DESIDERIUS ERASMUS: Erasmus and His Age: *Selected Letters. Edited with an Introduction by Hans J. Hillerbrand. Translated by Marcus A. Haworth* TB/1461
WALLACE K. FERGUSON et al.: Facets of the Renaissance TB/1098
WALLACE K. FERGUSON et al.: The Renaissance: *Six Essays. Illus.* TB/1084
FRANCESCO GUICCIARDINI: History of Florence. *Translated with an Introduction and Notes by Mario Domandi* TB/1470
WERNER L. GUNDERSHEIMER, Ed.: French Humanism, 1470-1600. * *Illus.* TB/1473
MARIE BOAS HALL, Ed.: Nature and Nature's Laws: *Documents of the Scientific Revolution #* HR/1420
HANS J. HILLERBRAND, Ed., The Protestant Reformation # TB/1342
JOHAN HUIZINGA: Erasmus and the Age of Reformation. *Illus.* TB/19
JOEL HURSTFIELD: The Elizabethan Nation TB/1312
JOEL HURSTFIELD, Ed.: The Reformation Crisis TB/1267
PAUL OSKAR KRISTELLER: Renaissance Thought: *The Classic, Scholastic, and Humanist Strains* TB/1048
PAUL OSKAR KRISTELLER: Renaissance Thought II: *Papers on Humanism and the Arts* TB/1163
PAUL O. KRISTELLER & PHILIP P. WIENER, Eds.: Renaissance Essays TB/1392
DAVID LITTLE: Religion, Order and Law: *A Study in Pre-Revolutionary England. § Preface by R. Bellah* TB/1418
NICCOLO MACHIAVELLI: History of Florence and of the Affairs of Italy: *From the Earliest Times to the Death of Lorenzo the Magnificent. Introduction by Felix Gilbert* TB/1027
ALFRED VON MARTIN: Sociology of the Renaissance. ° *Introduction by W. K. Ferguson* TB/1099
GARRETT MATTINGLY et al.: Renaissance Profiles. *Edited by J. H. Plumb* TB/1162
J. H. PARRY: The Establishment of the European Hegemony: 1415-1715: *Trade and Exploration in the Age of the Renaissance* TB/1045
J. H. PARRY, Ed.: The European Reconnaissance: *Selected Documents #* HR/1345
J. H. PLUMB: The Italian Renaissance: *A Concise Survey of Its History and Culture* TB/1161
A. F. POLLARD: Henry VIII. *Introductioh by A. G. Dickens.* ° TB/1249
RICHARD H. POPKIN: The History of Scepticism from Erasmus to Descartes TB/1391
PAOLO ROSSI: Philosophy, Technology, and the Arts, in the Early Modern Era 1400-1700. || *Edited by Benjamin Nelson. Translated by Salvator Attanasio* TB/1458

R. H. TAWNEY: The Agrarian Problem in the Sixteenth Century. *Intro. by Lawrence Stone* TB/1315

H. R. TREVOR-ROPER: The European Witch-craze of the Sixteenth and Seventeenth Centuries and Other Essays ° TB/1416

VESPASIANO: Rennaissance Princes, Popes, and *XVth Century: The Vespasiano Memoirs. Introduction by Myron P. Gilmore. Illus.* TB/1111

History: Modern European

RENE ALBRECHT-CARRIE, Ed.: The Concert of Europe # HR/1341

MAX BELOFF: The Age of Absolutism, 1660-1815 TB/1062

OTTO VON BISMARCK: Reflections and Reminiscences. *Ed. with Intro. by Theodore S. Hamerow* ¶ TB/1357

EUGENE C. BLACK, Ed.: British Politics in the Nineteenth Century # HR/1427

D. W. BROGAN: The Development of Modern France ° Vol. I: *From the Fall of the Empire to the Dreyfus Affair* TB/1184 Vol. II: *The Shadow of War, World War I, Between the Two Wars* TB/1185

ALAN BULLOCK: Hitler, A Study in Tyranny. ° *Revised Edition. Iuus.* TB/1123

GORDON A. CRAIG: From Bismarck to Adenauer: *Aspects of German Statecraft. Revised Edition* TB/1171

LESTER G. CROCKER, Ed.: The Age of Enlightenment # HR/1423

JACQUES DROZ: Europe between Revolutions, 1815-1848. ° *a Trans. by Robert Baldick* TB/1346

JOHANN GOTTLIEB FICHTE: Addresses to the German Nation. *Ed. with Intro. by George A. Kelly* ¶ TB/1366

ROBERT & ELBORG FORSTER, Eds.: European Society in the Eighteenth Century # HR/1404

C. C. GILLISPIE: Genesis and Geology: *The Decades before Darwin* § TB/51

ALBERT GOODWIN: The French Revolution TB/1064

JOHN B. HALSTED, Ed.: Romanticism # HR/1387

STANLEY HOFFMANN et al.: In Search of France: *The Economy, Society and Political System In the Twentieth Century* TB/1219

H. STUART HUGHES: The Obstructed Path: *French Social Thought in the Years of Desperation* TB/1451

JOHAN HUIZINGA: Dutch Civilisation in the 17th Century and Other Essays TB/1453

WALTER LAQUEUR & GEORGE L. MOSSE, Eds.: Education and Social Structure in the 20th Century. ° *Volume 6 of the* Journal of Contemporary History TB/1339

WALTER LAQUEUR & GEORGE L. MOSSE, Ed.: International Fascism, 1920-1945. ° *Volume 1 of the* Journal of Contemporary History TB/1276

WALTER LAQUEUR & GEORGE L. MOSSE, Eds.: Literature and Politics in the 20th Century. ° *Volume 5 of the* Journal of Contemporary History. TB/1328

WALTER LAQUEUR & GEORGE L. MOSSE, Eds.: The New History: *Trends in Historical Research and Writing Since World War II.* ° *Volume 4 of the* Journal of Contemporary History TB/1327

WALTER LAQUEUR & GEORGE L. MOSSE, Eds.: 1914: *The Coming of the First World War.* ° *Volume3 of the* Journal of Contemporary *History* TB/1306

JOHN MCMANNERS: European History, 1789-1914: *Men, Machines and Freedom* TB/1419

PAUL MANTOUX: The Industrial Revolution in the Eighteenth Century: *An Outline of the Beginnings of the Modern Factory System in England* TB/1079

KINGSLEY MARTIN: French Liberal Thought in the Eighteenth Century: *A Study of Political Ideas from Bayle to Condorcet* TB/1114

NAPOLEON III: Napoleonic Ideas: *Des Idées Napoléoniennes, par le Prince Napoléon-Louis Bonaparte. Ed. by Brison D. Gooch* ¶ TB/1336

FRANZ NEUMANN: Behemoth: *The Structure and Practice of National Socialism, 1933-1944* TB/1289

DAVID OGG: Europe of the Ancien Régime, 1715-1783 ° *a* TB/1271

GEORGE RUDE: Revolutionary Europe, 1783-1815 ° *a* TB/1272

MASSIMO SALVADORI, Ed.: Modern Socialism # TB/1374

DENIS MACK SMITH, Ed.: The Making of Italy, 1796-1870 # HR/1356

ALBERT SOREL: Europe Under the Old Regime, *Translated by Francis H. Herrick* TB/1121

ROLAND N. STROMBERG, Ed.: Realsim, Naturalism, and Symbolism: *Modes of Thought and Expression in Europe, 1848-1914* # HR/1355

A. J. P. TAYLOR: From Napoleon to Lenin: *Historical Essays* ° TB/1268

A. J. P. TAYLOR: The Habsburg Monarchy, 1809-1918: *A History of the Austrian Empire and Austria-Hungary* ° TB/1187

J. M. THOMPSON: European History, 1494-1789 TB/1431

DAVID THOMSON, Ed.: France: Empire and Republic, 1850-1940 # HR/1387

H. R. TREVOR-ROPER: Historical Essays TB/1269

W. WARREN WAGAR, Ed.: Science, Faith, and MAN: *European Thought Since 1914* # HR/1362

MACK WALKER, Ed.: Metternich's Europe, 1813-1848 # HR/1361

ELIZABETH WISKEMANN: Europe of the Dictators, 1919-1945 ° *a* TB/1273

JOHN B. WOLF: France: 1814-1919: *The Rise of a Liberal-Democratic Society* TB/3019

Literature & Literary Criticism

JACQUES BARZUN: The House of Intellect TB/1051

W. J. BATE: From Classic to Romantic: *Premises of Taste in Eighteenth Century England* TB/1036

VAN WYCK BROOKS: Van Wyck Brooks: The Early Years: *A Selection from his Works, 1908-1921 Ed. with Intro. by Claire Sprague* TB/3082

RICHMOND LATTIMORE, Translator: The Odyssey of Homer TB/1389

ROBERT PREYER, Ed.: Victorian Literature ** TB/1302

BASIL WILEY: Nineteenth Century Studies: *Coleridge to Matthew Arnold* ° TB/1261

RAYMOND WILLIAMS: Culture and Society, 1780-1950 ° TB/1252

Philosophy

HENRI BERGSON: Time and Free Will: *An Essay on the Immediate Data of Consciousness* ° TB/1021

LUDWIG BINSWANGER: Being-in-the-World: *Selected Papers. Trans. with Intro. by Jacob Needleman* TB/1365

H. J. BLACKHAM: Six Existentialist Thinkers: *Kierkegaard, Nietzsche, Jaspers, Marcel, Heidegger, Sartre* ° TB/1002

J. M. BOCHENSKI: The Methods of Contemporary Thought. *Trans. by Peter Caws* TB/1377
CRANE BRINTON: Nietzsche. *Preface, Bibliography, and Epilogue by the Author* TB/1197
ERNST CASSIRER: Rousseau, Kant and Goethe. *Intro. by Peter Gay* TB/1092
FREDERICK COPLESTON, *S. J.*: Medieval Philosophy TB/376
F. M. CORNFORD: From Religion to Philosophy: *A Study in the Origins of Western Speculation* § TB/20
WILFRID DESAN: The Tragic Finale: *An Essay on the Philosophy of Jean-Paul Sartre* TB/1030
MARVIN FARBER· The Aims of Phenomenology: *The Motives, Methods, and Impact of Husserl's Thought* TB/1291
PAUL FRIEDLANDER: Plato: *An Introduction* TB/2017
MICHAEL GELVEN: A Commentary on Heidegger's "Being and Time" TB/1464
J. GLENN GRAY: Hegel and Greek Thought TB/1409
W. K. C. GUTHRIE: The Greek Philosophers: *From Thales to Aristotle* ° TB/1008
G. W. F. HEGEL: On Art, Religion Philosophy: *Introductory Lectures to the Realm of Absolute Spirit. || Edited with an Introduction by J. Glenn Gray* TB/1463
G. W. F. HEGEL: Phenomenology of Mind. ° || *Introduction by George Lichtheim* TB/1303
MARTIN HEIDEGGER: Discourse on Thinking. *Translated with a Preface by John M. Anderson and E. Hans Freund. Introduction by John M. Anderson* TB/1459
F. H. HEINEMANN: Existentialism and the Modern Predicament TB/28
WERER HEISENBERG: Physics and Philosophy: *The Revolution in Modern Science. Intro. by F. S. C. Nortrop* TB/549
EDMUND HUSSERL: Phenomenology and the Crisis of Philosophy. § *Translated with an Introduction by Quentin Lauer* TB/1170
IMMANUEL KANT: Groundwork of the Metaphysic of Morals. *Translated and Analyzed by H. J. Paton* TB/1159
IMMANUEL KANT: Lectures on Ethics. § *Introduction by Lewis White Beck* TB/105
QUENTIN LAUER: Phenomenology: *Its Genesis and Prospect. Preface by Aron Gurwitsch* TB/1169
GEORGE A. MORGAN: What Nietzsche Means TB/1198
H. J. PATON: The Categorical Imperative: *A Study in Kant's Moral Philosophy* TB/1325
MICHAEL POLANYI: Personal Knowledge: *Towards a Post-Critical Philosophy* TB/1158
KARL R. POPPER: Conjectures and Refutations: *The Growth of Scientific Knowledge* TB/1376
WILLARD VAN ORMAN QUINE: Elementary Logic *Revised Edition* TB/577
MORTON WHITE: Foundations of Historical Knowledge TB/1440
WILHELM WINDELBAND: A History of Philosophy *Vol. I: Greek, Roman, Medieval* TB/38 *Vol. II: Renaissance, Enlightenment, Modern* TB/39
LUDWIG WITTGENSTEIN: The Blue and Brown Books ° TB/1211
LUDWIG WITTGENSTEIN: Notebooks, 1914-1916 TB/1441

Political Science & Government

C. E. BLACK: The Dynamics of Modernization: *A Study in Comparative History* TB/1321
KENNETH E. BOULDING: Conflict and Defense: *A General Theory of Action* TB/3024
DENIS W. BROGAN: Politics in America. *New Introduction by the Author* TB/1469
ROBERT CONQUEST: Power and Policy in the USSR: *The Study of Soviet Dynastics* ° TB/1307
ROBERT A. DAHL & CHARLES E. LINDBLOM: Politics, Economics, and Welfare: *Planning and Politico-Economic Systems Resolved into Basic Social Processes* TB/1277
HANS KOHN: Political Ideologies of the 20th Century TB/1277
ROY C. MACRIDIS, Ed.: Political Parties: *Contemporary Trends and Ideas* ** TB/1322
ROBERT GREEN MC CLOSKEY: American Conservatism in the Age of Enterprise, 1865-1910 TB/1137
BARRINGTON MOORE, JR.:Political Power and Social Theory: *Seven Studies* || TB/1221
BARRINGTON MOORE, JR.: Soviet Politics—The Dilemma of Power: *The Role of Ideas in Social Change* || TB/1222
BARRINGTON MOORE, JR.: Terror and Progress—USSR: *Some Sources of Change and Stability in the Soviet Dictatorship* TB/1266
JOHN B. MORRALL: Political Thought in Medieval Times TB/1076
KARL R. POPPER: The Open Society and Its Enemies *Vol. I: The Spell of Plato* TB/1101 *Vol. II: The High Tide of Prophecy: Hegel, Marx, and the Aftermath* TB/1102
HENRI DE SAINT-SIMON: Social Organization, The Science of Man, and Other Writings. || *Edited and Translated with an Introduction by Felix Markham* TB/1152
JOSEPH A. SCHUMPETER: Capitalism, Socialism and Democracy TB/3008

Psychology

LUDWIG BINSWANGER: Being-in-the-world: *Selected papers. || Trans. with Intro. by Jacob Needleman* TB/1365
HADLEY CANTRIL: The Invasion from Mars: *A Study in the Psychology of Panic* || TB/1282
MIRCEA ELIADE: Cosmos and History: *The Myth of the Eternal Return* § TB/2050
MIRCEA ELIADE: Myth and Reality TB/1369
MIRCEA ELIADE: Myths, Dreams and Mysteries: *The Encounter Between Contemporary Faiths and Archaic Realities* § TB/1320
MIRCEA ELIADE: Rites and Symbols of Initiation: *The Mysteries of Birth and Rebirth* § TB/1236
HERBERT FINGARETTE: The Self in Transformation: *Psychoanalysis, Philosophy and the Life of the Spirit* || TB/1177
SIGMUND FREUD: On Creativity and the Unconscious: *Papers on the Psychology of Art, Literature, Love, Religion.* § *Intro. by Benjamin Nelson* TB/45
J. GLENN GRAY: The Warriors: *Reflections on Men in Battle. Introduction by Hannah Arendt* TB/1294
WILLIAM JAMES: Psychology: *The Briefer Course. Edited with an Intro. by Gordon Allport* TB/1034
MUZAFER SHERIF: The Psychology of Social Norms. *Introduction by Gardner Murphy* TB/3072
HELLMUT WILHELM: Change: *Eight Lectures on the* I Ching TB/2019

Religion: Ancient and Classical, Biblical and Judaic Traditions

C. K. BARRETT, Ed.: The New Testament Background: *Selected Documents* TB/86

MARTIN BUBER: Eclipse of God: *Studies in the Relation Between Religion and Philosophy* TB/12

MARTIN BUBER: Hasidism and Modern Man. *Edited and Translated by Maurice Friedman* TB/839

MARTIN BUBER: The Knowledge of Man. *Edited with an Introduction by Maurice Friedman. Translated by Maurice Friedman and Ronald Gregor Smith* TB/135

MARTIN BUBER: Moses. *The Revelation and the Covenant* TB/837

MARTIN BUBER: The Origin and Meaning of Hasidism. *Edited and Translated by Maurice Friedman* TB/835

MARTIN BUBER: The Prophetic Faith TB/73

MARTIN BUBER: Two Types of Faith: *Interpenetration of Judaism and Christianity* ° TB/75

MALCOLM L. DIAMOND: Martin Buber: *Jewish Existentialist* TB/840

M. S. ENSLIN: Christian Beginnings TB/5

M. S. ENSLIN: The Literature of the Christian Movement TB/6

HENRI FRANKFORT: Ancient Egyptian Religion: *An Interpretation* TB/77

MAURICE S. FRIEDMAN: Martin Buber: *The Life of Dialogue* TB/64

ABRAHAM HESCHEL: The Earth Is the Lord's & The Sabbath. *Two Essays* TB/828

ABRAHAM HESCHEL: God in Search of Man: *A Philosophy of Judaism* TB/807

ABRAHAM HESCHEL: Man Is not Alone: *A Philosophy of Religion* TB/838

ABRAHAM HESCHEL: The Prophets: *An Introduction* TB/1421

T. J. MEEK: Hebrew Origins TB/69

JAMES MUILENBURG: The Way of Israel: *Biblical Faith and Ethics* TB/133

H. H. ROWLEY: The Growth of the Old Testament TB/107

D. WINTON THOMAS, Ed.: Documents from Old Testament Times TB/85

Religion: Early Christianity Through Reformation

ANSELM OF CANTERBURY: Truth, Freedom, and Evil: *Three Philosophical Dialogues. Edited and Translated by Jasper Hopkins and Herbert Richardson* TB/317

MARSHALL W. BALDWIN, Ed.: Christianity through the 13th Century # HR/1468

ADOLF DEISSMAN: Paul: *A Study in Social and Religious History* TB/15

EDGAR J. GOODSPEED: A Life of Jesus TB/1

ROBERT M. GRANT: Gnosticism and Early Christianity TB/136

WILLIAM HALLER: The Rise of Puritanism TB/22

ARTHUR DARBY NOCK: St. Paul ° TR/104

GORDON RUPP: Luther's Progress to the Diet of Worms ° TB/120

Religion: The Protestant Tradition

KARL BARTH: Church Dogmatics: *A Selection. Intro. by H. Gollwitzer. Ed. by G. W. Bromiley* TB/95

KARL BARTH: Dogmatics in Outline TB/56

KARL BARTH: The Word of God and the Word of Man TB/13

WHITNEY R. CROSS: The Burned-Over District: *The Social and Intellectual History of Enthusiastic Religion in Western New York, 1800-1850* TB/1242

WILLIAM R. HUTCHISON, Ed.: American Protestant Thought: *The Liberal Era* ‡ TB/1385

SOREN KIERKEGAARD: The Journals of Kierkegaard. ° *Edited with an Intro. by Alexander Dru* TB/52

SOREN KIERKEGAARD: The Point of View for My Work as an Author: *A Report to History.* § *Preface by Benjamin Nelson* TB/88

SOREN KIERKEGAARD: The Present Age. § *Translated and edited by Alexander Dru. Introduction by Walter Kaufmann* TB/94

SOREN KIERKEGAARD: Purity of Heart. *Trans. by Douglas Steere* TB/4

SOREN KIERKEGAARD: Repetition: *An Essay in Experimental Psychology* § TB/117

SOREN KIERKEGAARD: Works of Love: *Some Christian Reflections in the Form of Discourses* TB/122

WOLFHART PANNENBERG, et al.: History and Hermeneutic. *Volume 4 of* Journal for Theology and the Church, *edited by Robert W. Funk and Gerhard Ebeling* TB/254

F. SCHLEIERMACHER: The Christian Faith. *Introduction by Richard R. Niebuhr.* Vol. I TB/108; Vol. II TB/109

F. SCHLEIERMACHER: On Religion: *Speeches to Its Cultured Despisers. Intro. by Rudolf Otto* TB/36

PAUL TILLICH: Dynamics of Faith TB/42

PAUL TILLICH: Morality and Beyond TB/142

Religion: The Roman & Eastern Christian Traditions

A. ROBERT CAPONIGRI, Ed.: Modern Catholic Thinkers II: *The Church and the Political Order* TB/307

G. P. FEDOTOV: The Russian Religious Mind: *Kievan Christianity, the tenth to the thirteenth Centuries* TB/370

GABRIEL MARCEL: Being and Having: *An Existential Diary. Introduction by James Collins* TB/310

GABRIEL MARCEL: Homo Viator: *Introduction to a Metaphysic of Hope* TB/397

Religion: Oriental Religions

TOR ANDRAE: Mohammed: *The Man and His Faith* § TB/62

EDWARD CONZE: Buddhism: *Its Essence and Development.* ° *Foreword by Arthur Waley* TB/58

EDWARD CONZE: Buddhist Meditation TB/1442

EDWARD CONZE et al, Editors: Buddhist Texts through the Ages TB/113

ANANDA COOMARASWAMY: Buddha and the Gospel of Buddhism TB/119

H. G. CREEL: Confucius and the Chinese Way TB/63

FRANKLIN EDGERTON, Trans. & Ed.: The Bhagavad Gita TB/115

SWAMI NIKHILANANDA, Trans. & Ed.: The Upanishads TB/114

Religion: Philosophy, Culture, and Society

NICOLAS BERDYAEV: The Destiny of Man TB/61

RUDOLF BULTMANN: History and Eschatology: *The Presence of Eternity* ° TB/91

RUDOLF BULTMANN AND FIVE CRITICS: Kerygma and Myth: *A Theological Debate* TB/80

RUDOLF BULTMANN and KARL KUNDSIN: Form search. *Trans. by F. C. Grant* TB/96

LUDWIG FEUERBACH: The Essence of Christianity. § *Introduction by Karl Barth. Foreword by H. Richard Niebuhr* TB/11

KYLE HASELDEN: The Racial Problem in Christian Perspective TB/116

MARTIN HEIDEGGER: Discourse on Thinking. *Translated with a Preface by John M. Anderson and E. Hans Freund. Introduction by John M. Anderson* TB/1459
IMMANUEL KANT: Religion Within the Limits of Reason Alone. § *Introduction by Theodore M. Greene and John Silber* TB/FG
H. RICHARD NIERUHR: Christ and Culture TB/3
H. RICHARD NIEBUHR: The Kingdom of God in America TB/49
JOHN H. RANDALL, JR.: The Meaning of Religion for Man. *Revised with New Intro. by the Author* TB/1379

Science and Mathematics

W. E. LE GROS CLARK: The Antecedents of Man: *An Introduction to the Evolution of the Primates.* ° *Illus.* TB/559
ROBERT E. COKER: Streams, Lakes, Ponds. *Illus.* TB/586
ROBERT E. COKER: This Great and Wide Sea: *An Introduction to Oceanography and Marine Biology. Illus.* TB/551
F. K. HARE: The Restless Atmosphere TB/560
WILLARD VAN ORMAN QUINE: Mathematical Logic TB/558

Science: Philosophy

J. M. BOCHENSKI: The Methods of Contemporary Thought. *Tr. by Peter Caws* TB/1377
J. BRONOWSKI: Science and Human Values. *Revised and Enlarged. Illus.* TB/505
WERNER HEISENBERG: Physics and Philosophy: *The Revolution in Modern Science. Introduction by F. S. C. Northrop* TB/549
KARL R. POPPER: Conjectures and Refutations: *The Growth of Scientific Knowledge* TB/1376
KARL R. POPPER: The Logic of Scientific Discovery TB/576

Sociology and Anthropology

REINHARD BENDIX: Work and Authority in Industry: *Ideologies of Management in the Course of Industrialization* TB/3035
BERNARD BERELSON, Ed., The Behavioral Sciences Today TB/1127
KENNETH B. CLARK: Dark Ghetto: *Dilemmas of Social Power. Foreword by Gunnar Myrdal* TB/1317
KENNETH CLARK & JEANNETTE HOPKINS: A Relevant War Against Poverty: *A Study of Community Action Programs and Observable Social Change* TB/1480
LEWIS COSER, Ed.: Political Sociology TB/1293
ROSE L. COSER, Ed.: Life Cycle and Achievement in America ** TB/1434
ALLISON DAVIS & JOHN DOLLARD: Children of Bondage: *The Personality Development of Negro Youth in the Urban South* || TB/3049
ST. CLAIR DRAKE & HORACE R. CAYTON: Black Metropolis: *A Study of Negro Life in a Northern City. Introduction by Everett C. Hughes. Tables, maps, charts, and graphs* Vol. I TB/1086; Vol. II TB/1087
PETER F. DRUCKER: The New Society: *The Anatomy of Industrial Order* TB/1082
LEON FESTINGER, HENRY W. RIECKEN, STANLEY SCHACHTER: When Prophecy Fails: *A Social and Psychological Study of a Modern Group that Predicted the Destruction of the World* || TB/1132
CHARLES Y. GLOCK & RODNEY STARK: Christian Beliefs and Anti-Semitism. *Introduction by the Authors* TB/1454
L. S. B. LEAKEY: Adam's Ancestors: *The Evolution of Man and His Culture. Illus.* TB/1019
KURT LEWIN: Field Theory in Social Science: *Selected Theoretical Papers.* || *Edited by Dorwin Cartwright* TB/1135
RITCHIE P. LOWRY: Who's Running This Town? *Community Leadership and Social Change* TB/1383
R. M. MACIVER: Social Causation TB/1153
GARY T. MARX: Protest and Prejudice: *A Study of Belief in the Black Community* TB/1435
ROBERT K. MERTON, LEONARD BROOM, LEONARD S. COTTRELL, JR., Editors: Sociology Today: *Problems and Prospects* || Vol. I TB/1173; Vol. II TB/1174
GILBERT OSOFSKY, Ed.: The Burden of Race: A Documentary History of Negro-White Relations in America TB/1405
GILBERT OSOFSKY: Harlem: The Making of a Ghetto: *Negro New York 1890-1930* TB/1381
TALCOTT PARSONS & EDWARD A. SHILS, Editors: Toward a General Theory of Action: *Theoretical Foundations for the Social Sciences* TB/1083
PHILIP RIEFF: The Triumph of the Therapeutic: *Uses of Faith After Freud* TB/1360
JOHN H. ROHRER & MUNRO S. EDMONSON, Eds.: The Eighth Generation Grows Up: *Cultures and Personalities of New Orleans Negroes* || TB/3050
ARNOLD ROSE: The Negro in America: *The Condensed Version of Gunnar Myrdal's* An American Dilemma. *Second Edition* TB/3048
GEORGE ROSEN: Madness in Society: *Chapters in the Historical Sociology of Mental Illness.* || *Preface by Benjamin Nelson* TB/1337
PHILIP SELZNICK: TVA and the Grass Roots: *A Study in the Sociology of Formal Organization* TB/1230
PITIRIM A. SOROKIN: Contemporary Sociological Theories: *Through the First Quarter of the Twentieth Century* TB/3046
MAURICE R. STEIN: The Eclipse of Community: *An Interpretation of American Studies* TB/1128
FERDINAND TONNIES: Community and Society: *Gemeinschaft und Gesellschaft. Translated and Edited by Charles P. Loomis* TB/1116
SAMUEL E. WALLACE: Skid Row as a Way of Life TB/1367
W. LLOYD WARNER and Associates: Democracy in Jonesville: *A Study in Quality and Inequality* || TB/1129
W. LLOYD WARNER: Social Class in America: *The Evaluation of Status* TB/1013
FLORIAN ZNANIECKI: The Social Role of the Man of Knowledge. *Introduction by Lewis A. Coser* TB/1372

71 72 73 74 12 11 10 9 8 7 6 5 4 3 2 1